From Plantation to the Pulpit

The Transforming Message of the Black Baptist Church

"The Life of William Henry Murphy, Sr."

Compiled and Written By
Paris Lee Smith

Foreword

From Plantation to the Pulpit
The Life of William Henry
Murphy, Sr.

...What manner of man is this that, even the wind and the sea obey him?
St. Mark 4: 41b

You have heard the story before. Jesus found himself on a boat with his Disciples in the middle of a storm. Because they became fearful, the Disciples awaken Jesus who immediately arose and spoke to the sea, "**Peace be still**," and the wind ceased and there was a great calm. Jesus amazed even his Disciples, these up close and personal followers, as he spoke to the elements and commanded obedience. The sea calmed. Indeed, what manner of Man is this?

My friend, the Reverend Paris Lee Smith, Sr. has scripted with passion an unmatched accounting of the life of this giant of a man, the Reverend Doctor William Henry Murphy, Sr. This is, indeed, a story that will touch your heart, expand your intellect, and provide a road map to achieve your goals under the Lord's leadership. I applaud the skill of Paris in penning this biographical work and I admire and applaud the life of this special Man of God, the Reverend Murphy. <u>From Plantation to the Pulpit—The Life of William Henry Murphy, Sr.</u> has an identity connection for each person who chooses to read it. If your childhood is not a replica of perfection, then this is the book for you. If you had a significant other in your life that protected and loved you unconditionally, like Grandmother, then this book is for you.

If you want to understand how the church and the powerful Gospel message can become life-sustaining factors in the day-to-day experiences in a life, then this is surely a book for you. If you want to see how the life choices of one special, godly man can effect positive change for thousands, then this is the book for you. If you need to be re-energized by the fact that even if the plantation is your location for a time in your life, it does not have to be your permanent home. You can move from a life of subjugation to one of total and complete liberation physically and spiritually under the Lord. Dr. Murphy leads the way.

Throughout these intriguing pages, I am continually reminded and brought back to the passage in St. Mark. What manner of man is this? What manner of man is this that in his finite, but a second of a journey here on earth has been able to move to and through many storms to safety in His arms. Reverend Doctor William Henry Murphy, Sr., lead on! Show us the way! You are the man!

-Dr. William T. Perkins-

Foreword

Not many people have the opportunity to experience and be a part of a great legacy as the Murphy family. To be a part of four generations of living William Murphy's is unbelievable. I am so blessed to be a part of what God is doing within this family through this mighty man of God.

As you read the pages of this writing, what will unfold before your eyes is the "all" that it takes to become what God has called you to do in this life. That becoming is not easy. What seemly should be easy, because God has purposed it in the spirit is many times a struggle and much travail. It reminds us of the pain that a woman bears to bring forth life even though it is a blessing; it costs to bring forth life. As Dr. Murphy releases his story and the wisdom that has come through the life that he has lived, one will come to know that it has not been easy, but that there was a great price, that had to be paid!

This is one of the most powerful writings of this day because of the contents within shared from the writer. All that I am, is rooted and grounded in the spiritual wisdom and strength of my hero and pastor. If ever there is a life that needs transcended to the pages, I believe that it is the life of Dr. William H. Murphy Sr.

-Bishop William H. Murphy, Jr.-

Preface

〜

G erald Lamont Thomas helps us with this understanding: "In the African oral tradition of sharing wisdom with the generations to come, many of the homeland traditions, practices, and rituals are infused into the fiber of the African American religious experience." It is from this reality that we are attempting to share a black Baptist faith story and testimony of faith. From the residue of slavery being present in the spirit of a paternal grandmother, she instills into the character of her grandson, a faith in the Almighty God, who holds them anchored during a time that is so intense with racism and inhumanity to the people of color. Many of these stories will continue to go untold and forgotten because many of the people have left these mundane shores. Therefore, while the dew is still fresh in the photographic memory of this man of faith, we launch this project to shed light upon his rich history in the black Baptist church experience. Life will cause people's lives to cross and in the walk, many lives are intercorrelated and in this work, the author is the humble recipient of a gracious plectrum of a black Baptist preacher's lives and ministries. The author himself becomes over -whelmed with the adventure of this man of God's story, that he shares a commentary through the texture of the testimony as he receives the story firsthand. The man of faith walks through life with the apprehension of the times, but with the steady beat of hope and destiny beckoning upon his spirit. Therefore, the beat goes on...!

Acknowledgements

⟞⟝

To my late grandmother, Willie Ruth Beden, who served many years as an usher at the New Bethel Baptist Church of Detroit, Michigan under the late C.L. Franklin during the church's days on Hastings Street, that I first witnessed the faith of a woman in God. It was her keen insight that I remember her telling me as a little boy that she saw me as a lawyer or a judge; although she never heard me preach, but when I stand behind that holy pulpit, I sense her presence in my bosom to make something out of myself. Thank God for the black Baptist church.

I would like to personally thank Pastor Alvin M. Ballinger, Sr., whose intentional efforts to share the gospel in the Northland Mall of Southfield, Michigan during a time when hanging out was the order of the day. Pastor Ballinger, whom is my "Andrew", told me to come and see. It is to him, I owe a grand debt of gratitude for meeting my "Father in the ministry" Pastor William Henry Murphy, Sr. Thanks brother man! There are numerous members of the Greater Ebenezer Missionary Baptist Church family, past and present that have contributed to my life as a son of the black Baptist church. I sincerely thank them!

To my writing assistant, Ms. Sandra K. Fortner of Louisville, Kentucky whose writing skills and dictation abilities are priceless. Her words of comfort and consolation to finish this enormous project have served as a catalyst to thrust me to the finalization.

Finally, please allow me to officially thank, Dr. William Henry Murphy, Sr., for his humble submission of sharing the intimate details of his life, with me and now the world at large. I am indebted to you personally for your love, patience, faith, encouragement, discipline, tenacity, nuggets of wisdom, and longsuffering you have displayed towards me as we walked this joyful journey of "Walking by faith, and not by sight" together these past twenty-seven years. No matter what state I have found myself in personally and ministerially, you have been an unmovable strong tower to lean upon. "Dad", I love you man! My hope is that you will know that by this demonstration of love. I humbly and graciously submit this story. *Lord, enlarge our territory for your Glory!*

-Paris Lee Smith-

Introduction

⌇

The wealth and depth of a rich cultural experience lives in its ability to retain some of the essential experiences it has nestled within its bosom. This cultural experience lives in the fabric and fiber of the black Baptist church. With a plurality in the world today of religious experiences and places of worship, there is a unique distinctive feature about this cultural ecclesiastical representative that carries with it a story of relevance and revelation. In the history of the black Baptist Church, a dynamic, rich heritage experience emerges a giant, a giant in faith and a giant in the power of belief in God almighty. This story will be unfolded in the pages of this book, in some detail, the survival of a man who embraces the promise of God and a promise to his paternal grandmother, to make something out of himself. We share this history with the world with humility to show forth the glorious work of faith in the life of a man whose upbringing is cultivated in the black Baptist church experience and a faith in God infused into his bosom from the life of trusting in the Lord, he witnessed in the life of his grandmother. He gladly opens his heart to include the world at large, to the reality that the power of God can do in one's life. Only when we succumb to the understanding that only a God, can take time and use it as an incubator to birth promise and potential into a person's life and give them the tenacity to "walk by faith, and not by sight."

This transforming message, we share in the title, is the kind of autobiography and biography, which this world we believe is begging to hear about, that is true to its intent and not filled with an overabundance of fabrication or puffed egotistical jargon. This is filled with the admiration of a son, for a father in the life of the black Baptist church. In the tradition of the African culture, is the oral tradition of sharing one's faith with the future generations. It is what the elders do in light of sharing some wisdom for life's journey. The father we speak of is none other than, Dr. William Henry Murphy, Sr.

In the year of 1980, during a critical time in the author's life, he stumbled into a church, sitting on the avenue of Fenkell Street, in the city of Detroit, (his hometown and stumping ground) with a well manicured lawn and picturesque flower beds, a new world of exposure, and a new dawn to the horizons of his life. Sitting next to a nurse, dressed in white, a few pews from the door, facing the choir, the young understudy studies the giant, with his gestures and gyrations of his demonstrative expression of the gospel message, the young fellow sits in uncertainty and with a sense of belonging. With bubbles in his stomach he hears a melodious choir and a message that was to become the beginning of a transformation in his life from a preacher who was so convincing in his delivery, that this young seventeen year old, got up and gave this man of God his hand and gave God his heart. This is why we are telling this story, because this is transformation in its infancy, for when the Gospel is preached and taught, it shall raise one up out of their seat and thrust them into the process of transformation and redemption. William H. Murphy, Sr. is this man of God and giant of a man that has survived the days of the plantation in the foothills of the Tennessee valley, endured being called, somebody's boy, who now sits in the office of the daughter for the Lord Jesus, Greater Ebenezer Missionary Baptist Church, sharing his life with the author. This is proof that a "walk of faith" is a life that can be examined for the sake of empowerment to fuel the lives of others who are faced with some unbelievable odds stacked against them.

The writer of this autobiography and biography brings twenty-seven years of his own life into the pages of this book, while openly sharing this history with all who would listen to this heartfelt story. This dynamic, cultural, life changing experience, we believe will help encourage those who feel that life has nothing to offer but only a fantasy of reality, but that life has a purpose, a plan, and a powerful pilgrimage of faith that needs someone to walk in the footsteps that have been ordered by the Lord. The author sits in the classes of the Interdenominational Theological Center in Atlanta, Georgia, under the banner of the Morehouse School of Religion, filled with the excitement of a kid in a toy store, remembering where he sits, as a testimony of the transforming message, he received a quarter of a century ago at the bosom of Pastor William H. Murphy, Sr. It was in the Baptist History class taught by Dr. J. Sherman Pelt, that the author listened to the history of the Baptist church and understood the magnitude of his own black Baptist history was cultivated and nurtured in the bosom of this giant for God; he was inspired to write about this man of God. When we say "giant," we are suggesting that a person can have giant size faith and not be a physical giant. William Henry has exhibited a tremendous faith in tough times and has given to the Christian faith and the black Baptist church a testimony of faith.

Although many great preachers and scholars have coached the author, none of these can truly claim him as their son of thunder, yet they are included in this work, as for the clarity they offer to the further understanding of the message he initially received.

Two "Sons of Thunder" which are given special recognition, because of the impact and training they afforded the author in the life of this transformation during its infancy, Pastor Alvin Ballinger, Sr., of St. Mark Baptist Church of Columbus, Ohio, whom was the author's "Andrew" in that he invited him to the church. Pastor Ballinger exhibited the rare virtue of service to Dr. Murphy that has not been duplicated by none other son of the spirit. Bishop William H. Murphy, Jr., who goes from "Billy to Bishop" has never rejected or denied the integrity of the fellowship of the "Sons of Thunder." He is and has been a lifestyle coach to all, and especially to the author. It is Bishop Murphy's goodwill that the author holds dear to his life. He shares intimately his life with us all who tried to understand his father's drive and ambition for excellence, that he has well established himself as a true "branch" of his father's loins, as well as a father to his family in the flesh, but to all of the sons he is now "fathering" in the spirit.

They bring clarity to the transforming message with their messages and help bring the "Bud" to full bloom. Bishop Murphy is without a doubt a living testimony to the life of faith and the transforming message of the black Baptist church. His life has offered to all the "Sons of Thunder" the example it takes to follow the leading of the Holy Spirit in the life of a preacher called by God for a certain season in their life according to God's divine mandate. Pastor Ballinger gives us hope, despite how hopeless a situation appears, God still has the last word. All we need is a word from the Lord!

The following Pastors and preachers have helped encourage the author through their lives, preaching, and theological aptitude as well as have many allowed the author to share his attempts to preach the gospel. Pastors Willie R. Campbell, Edgar L. Vann, Sr., Sampson Matthews, Bishop J. Douglas Wiley, Bishop Otis Floyd, Dr. Gardner C. Taylor, Dr. Joseph Jordan, Dr. Jim Holley, Dr. Joel Anthony Ward,

Professor Dr. Mark Lomax, Dr. Carolyn Knight, Dr.Tellis J. Chapman, Dr. Abraham Smith, Pastor Alvin Jackson, Sr., Pastor Maurice Jackson, Dr. Oscar King, III., Dr. Riggins R. Earl, Jr., Dr. A. Louis Patterson, Sr., Drs. Henry and Ella Mitchell, Dr. C.A.W.Clark, President Dr. Michael Battle, Dr. Frederick Douglass Haynes, III., Dr. Ralph Douglass West, Sr., Dr. R. L. White, Dr. Otis N. White, Pastor William E. Harris, Pastor E. Dewey Smith, Jr., Elder Charles L. Webb, the late Bishop David Ellis, Dr. Carl Hughes, Dr. Samuel Dewitt Proctor, Dr. Herbert Robinson, Dr. Charles Butler, Dr. Miles Jones, Dr. E. V. Hill, Dr. E. K. Bailey, Dr. Frederick G. Sampson, and Dr. Manuel Scott, Sr. and without a doubt C.L. Franklin and Dr. Martin Luther King, Jr., are all a part of this original message becoming clear and empowering for the transformation.

Dr. Allen B. Green of Erie, PA whose insight and encouraging words of comfort and wisdom are still to this day an anchor of hope and a relentless prodding upon the spirit to never lose faith in tough times and to trust God's providence even when one cannot sense the trace of his assurance. His investment is without a doubt, priceless.

Many thanks to Dr. John W. Kinney, Dean of the Samuel Dewitt Proctor School of Theology, whose out of the "box" approach to the "whole mind" theology and understanding of the Holy Ghost's anointing and presence in one's life is without a doubt a royal jewel that is treasured. Dr. Kinney thank you for allowing me to glean from the field of your ministry those essentials to pursue theological training and philosophical understandings of the full Gospel.

Special thanks to Dr.William T. Perkins, who has served as a mentor, friend, Dean, and theological coach as President of the Morehouse School of Religion at the Interdenominational Theological Center in Atlanta, Georgia. It has been the untiring love and devotion that, Dr. Perkins has shared in long hours of consultation and coaching the author still receives on a regular basis that keeps the author focused on the plan and purpose God has ordained from the beginning of his walk on the campuses of ITC.

Dr. J. Sherman Pelt, of Atlanta, GA, professor of "Baptist History and Baptist Polity," at ITC, whose convicting lectures and intimate dialogue concerning the magnificent contributions that the black Baptist church has given to the faith of Christianity, is the anchor of wisdom that should be invested in every black Baptist denominational representative. Be blessed, Dr. Pelt.

Dr. Cleopatrick Lacy of Griffin, Georgia shared with us the importance of keeping the integrity of the social gospel alive and vibrant as we seek to do ministry in the days ahead. Thanks, Dr. Lacy.

Dr. Edward Lee Branch of Detroit, MI, has been without a doubt an academic Pastor for us for many years. Dr. Branch licensed the author from his pulpit in Detroit to help authenticate the calling to the preaching ministry that was "budding" at a very important junction in the author's life. He placed structure in many sermonic presentations and to my life as a black Baptist preacher. Thanks, brother!

Sincere thanks goes to Dr. Jeremiah A. Wright, Jr. of Chicago, Ill. for his "theological and lifestyle coaching" and his many letters of encouragement and instructions for life, through some very tough and tight times in the life of the author. Thank you for tough love and your mentoring presence. Love you, man! Thanks Dr. Wright!

Yet God, in His infinite wisdom has afforded the author to share and be coached, by his present Pastor, Dr. Kevin W. Cosby at the St. Stephen Baptist Church and President of Simmons College of Louisville, both in Louisville, Kentucky. It has been through his sermonic presentations and Bible study on Wednesdays evenings that Dr. Kevin W. Cosby has given new life to this work. His passion for the people of color and his fuel to make positive change happen is rather bold, radical, and courageous, therefore it is inspirationally empowering. His mentoring of "iron sharpens iron" has allowed one to be thyself in the display of giftings. Thank you Dr. Cosby!

The author is a true Baptist preacher who appreciates the magnitude of this work and honestly and humbly submits it to the world for faith that is within the black Baptist church and it's message of hope, in these faithless times. We hope that in our finite efforts to tell this story, we be forgiven for not being perfect in our attempts. We pray God's blessing on the message of the book and on the intent it carries to the world at large, but primarily to the recognition to the power and influence of the black Baptist church and its message of hope.

-PLS-

Dedication Page
December 14, 2005
This treatise of my autobiography has risen from the depth of obscurity. However, because of the astuteness, dedication, love, and determination of one of my sons in the faith, Pastor/ Elder Paris Lee Smith, a young man in whom I take much pride in. His penmanship is unique and his thought pattern is prolific in style, which should make a great contribution to the kingdom of heaven.

Therefore I am indebted to Pastor/ Elder Paris Lee Smith, for his grand expression of respect, love, and appreciation that he has exemplified for me; it is to him and his lovely assistant, Sandra K. Fortner that I dedicate this thesis, and of course Dr. J. Sherman Pelt for planting the seed, Dr. William T. Perkins, Dean for your faithful support and faith in our son, and the faculty of Morehouse School of Religion at the ITC of Atlanta, Georgia.

In addition, to my servants, armor bearers, friends, and secretaries Sister Nicole Price and Sis. Kristen Parks. Praise God for your untiring work to accomplish this thesis.

To Mama Murphy, my love of fifty-six years and friend, who labored with me to achieve all, (whatever) and to my complete family in the flesh and spirit.

Therefore to my only son in the flesh, Bishop William H. Murphy Jr. Regional Bishop of the Full Gospel Fellowship, to William H. Murphy III for his artistic contributions to the kingdom of our Lord Jesus Christ, and William H. Murphy IV who just turned ten years old. To my five daughters, Carla, Carolyn, Debra, Pamara, and Alita and all the grandchildren and great grandchildren.

My hat is off to all the Ebenezians for your undaunted patience and support in every way.

1st Corinthians 15:58

"Therefore, my beloved brethren we are steadfast, unmovable, always abounding in the work of the Lord forasmuch as ye know that our Labours is not in vain in the Lord."

Yours in Divine Love

Dr. William H. Murphy Sr.,

The Plantation Experience

It has been suggested, that what we are and how we behave are the by-products of our childhood experiences we encounter. Many times those whom do not understand our passion in life judge us wrongly. In the childhood experiences of William Henry Murphy there is undoubtedly an incubator of childhood, yet very painful, a theological perspective that molded his character and placed within the bosom of his soul, the undeniable pursuit to live life with a sense of ethic and pride. He was forced into the reality of racism at the very tender age of seven years old with the man of the house responsibility and accountability. He shares the plantation experience from this perspective that allows the heart to feel the thrust of reality placed upon his spirit and his body.

Dr. Murphy shares his experiences, "Truly it was a phenomenal experience for me to have lived on the cutting edge of reconstruction on a plantation. For me as a boy raised on a plantation, subjected to the wishes and commands of the master or the owner of the plantation, was in many instances the same as slavery, if not worse." He holds to the notion that slavery was also a mental as well as a physical reality because if one succumbs to the tactics of slavery, then once the body weakens to the brutal treatment, then the only thing left was the spirit or the soul of a man. Liberation was at the outset for William Henry. He was destined to survive with the hope of God resting in his bosom. This is where the hope of the Gospel begins to germinate its seed in the spirit of the young boy, William Henry. He often detested the slothfulness of preachers working at the church in Detroit at Greater Ebenezer Missionary Baptist Church.

He would scold us preachers very hard at times, because in his spirit, he still carried the fact that laziness was not an option. Being raised by his grandmother and having an uncle who was verbally abused by the plantation owner, William Henry had to carry the load of a man at the tender age of seven years old. The hope of his grandmother, was the obligation to meet the demands of the master. Grandma lived through some brutal experiences as a child and young woman with the hope of God residing in her soul that one day the Lord would either deliver them from the plantation or restore a right relationship between the master and the servant. Therefore many years at harvest time, they would not even get paid for all the hard work they done all year. Dr. Murphy recalls the painful past, "Grandmother and I hardly ever received any compensation for our labor in the fields, other than what we could eat and many times that was scarce. Often I returned home from school to find no food. Grandmother would try to put together something for me to eat and many times it consisted of peaches, blackberries and cornbread, meat was a luxury." Dr. Murphy recalls the painful reality of the treatment that he received at the hands of those who ran the plantation and how this has affected his outlook on life. He has always presented himself as a product of excellence in that with a sense of godly reverence, he has tried to infuse in all he has encountered to beat the odds that were stacked up against them.

"Well, as a boy growing up on the plantation, of course on the cutting edge of reconstruction in America was not as terrible or dangerous or even life threatening as C. Eric Lincoln relates in his book entitled *"Coming through the*

Fire" Pg 22 –25. Mr. Lincoln relates his encounter with a gin manager who was a stately tall red-faced white man who always moved a cigar stub plunging into the corners of his mouth. The man automatically stomped his head, kicked him in the face, and stumbled his heavy broke ass and each kick was palm shaded as Mr. Lincoln puts it with an oath of profanity and the word nigger. He complained about the incident they coming in here going to teach me how to count cotton money. The redneck explained. Another four words of profanity and the embarrassing word nigger telling me how to count money, telling me I've done made a mistake. Oh my goodness gracious what a terrible incident that was. Anyway, my experience as a boy growing up I never had any encounters with white folks to that extent in TN not withstanding I'm sure there were many such encounters. There are several reasons as to why I never encountered such. One thing was that grandmother protected me and kept me from getting into such encounters."

"Grandmother was very witty. I remember the plantation owner Mr. David Moore who was a big seven footer. He called me one beautiful summer afternoon and commanded me to saddle Miss Julie's horse and saddle me one, as we road towards our little hut, grandmother was standing in front of the house with her hands on her hips. I knew then as I saw her that something was seriously happening. As soon as Miss Julie and I reached grandmother she yelled at me, "Boy get off that horse and carry him back to the stable." The way she said it no questions was necessary. I knew she meant what she said. What I was not aware of was that there were several white boys from the adjoining plantation riding towards us on their horses. Grandmother saw them and knew that meant trouble so she avoided the possibilities of me getting into trouble with those boys by riding with that white girl. So I immediately carried the horse back to the stable."

One thing that made our labors of survival more difficult on many of the plantations was the straw boss, Old Man Charlie Walker. He was a real charcoal black man with silvery gray hair. He was a raw hider commissioned by the plantation owner to always get the best out of each farm hand at all cost. If we were chopping cotton, he would get a hoe and lead the whole pack and everybody must keep up with him. That is if we expected to get paid. If we were picking cotton, or pulling corn, gathering peas, beans, tomatoes or whatever, Old Man Walker as a straw boss made sure we were doing our very best and whatever Old Man Straw Boss Walker said was law and order. I remember one Saturday morning I had an acre of ground I needed to finish plowing. I went to the stable to get me a mule or a horse of my choosing; preferably, one of the speedy horses or mule. I inadvertently picked Old Jack one of the best in the stable. However, Old Man Charlie saw me. He saw me bridling him, bridling Old Jack and that was his favorite mule.

Therefore, he would not permit me to use him. I was so disappointed, discouraged I ran back home to tell grandmother. I was mad and crying of course. Grandmother was excited wanting to know what was wrong with me. When I finished telling her the story, she headed for the Big House and related the incident to Mr. Dave Moore the owner. I was one of Mr. Moore's favorite niggas. He said so himself. He would often tell his friends "that's my nigga." "I raised that nigga." So he screamed down from the Big House "Charlie let that boy have that mule." There were several reasons Mr. Moore took a liking to me. First, I have always been a perfectionist, believing that things ought to be done just right. Mr. Moore saw that. When I plowed a row and if it was not straight, I would go over it until it was. I always had been like that about all things."

"My grandmother was exceptionally witty and strong, a strong woman. She took me in her home when I was approximately seven years old. At the time, she was living with her eldest son and I became man of the house at age seven. Being man of the house at age seven was a tremendous responsibility at such a young age. It meant milking the cows, feeding the hogs, cutting wood for cooking and warmth. Not only was the responsibility great, but also not knowing how to take care of myself, at such a young age made it even worse. For instance, the cow stepped upon my foot while milking her and made tremendous gashes on the top of my foot, which became frost bitten. This made it very difficult to heal, so I could not wear a shoe for quite some time. I truly realized what God was doing with me. I remember about eleven years old I hitched up a team of mules and wagon and went deep into the woods to cut down a load of wood for firewood to load on the wagon. In the process, I cut down a tree that was so heavy for me to lift and put it on the wagon. I should have cut the log in small pieces, but in order to expedite time because of darkness approaching, I failed to do so. I picked the end of the log up to the wagon wheel and accidentally wedged my hand under the log, which was humanly impossible to release. I had not the strength to lift that log off my hand, "My Lord." I stood there crying indeed, praying that God would help me raise that log up off my hand, for there was no one else in sight. What an experience that was for a child.

I not only learned the power and meaning of prayer but I learned to trust God who loves and cares. I received power from heaven into my right hand to lift that three hundred pound log off my hand. That incident convinced me of the truth that God works miracles."

"Well, black children growing up on a plantation were very limited as to play and educational opportunities. There were such games as hopscotch, jacks, and old gray horse. If you had some pecans, indeed or baseball even and we could not play either of those games on Sunday because of respect for the day of the Lord. That was a no-no. Educationally in the decade of the twentieth and thirtieth centuries through the forties, farming took up preeminence over education. During the thirties and forties most of the time I went to school a half day and worked in the fields the other half. But I was determined to accommodate, accumulate at all cost to acquire an education. As the late Dr. W. Hobart Brewster who once penned, "I was determined to be somebody some day." So I succeeded each year with top honors in spite of the difficulties. In my day those many things that were limited to relating to play, education etc. in the limitless gave place for the religious activities. We had time to attend church, which was the greatest contribution to our destiny. At church, we were privileged to meet and fellowship with old friends and relatives that we had not seen in a while. We were privileged, as children to run over the church grounds and have fun, "Praise the Lord." At church, the children were taught to respect the inner court such as worship, the pastor, our elder, indeed all motivated by respect and love for God. If you as a child wanted your ears pulled or a real hard pinch on the arm or chin just get out of line and you had it coming. But it was in this unique experience that granted me the necessary Christian fundamentals that God had predestined me to come, "Praise the Lord."

C. Eric Lincoln shares in his book, "This Road Since Freedom" pages 21-25 says, "The painful reality of being beaten physically by the master because he felt as though he got paid less than what was agreed upon. He was informed that no black boy could ever count behind a white man." Unlike C. Eric Lincoln's experience, William Henry's disposition was quite different, as it related to the unfair practices or physical tactics used to control blacks in the South, he would have defended his honor in a different way with force because of the past he experienced.

This experience is within the fiber of William Henry's personhood from the plantation experiences he endured with the shadows looming over his horizons for the plans in his life. He briefly shares the "straw boss" experience: "The task of the strawboss was to make the freed blacks that worked on the plantation to become more enslaved to his mistreatment of their lives by demonstrating their ability to maintain their sense of control by proving the workers as incapable of keeping up with his speed of labor. These hired hands were gathered from the Memphis area and brought to the plantation to work under conditions that were a lot harsher than the previous experiences of the slaves." Dr. Murphy recalls the one incident that stands out in his mind, he says during a phone conversation, "Son and that is the evening I came home from school and having an acre of land to plow, I was denied the right to use the best mule to plow from the strawboss and I was furiously upset that my grandmother went up to the Mr. Moore's big house to get him to release the best plow and mule for me to finish my work, he hollered down the hill to the strawboss to give me what I needed to get the job done, and he did just that." This is the kind of realities he had to face everyday of his youth while trying to finish school. His attitude and desire for excellence was clearly seen in his relentless pursuit for education. He knew deep down in the depths of his soul that education would give him the key or keys to survive and progress in life. His heart ached with the desire to leave the plantation and the only way out was the way up in education. His delight was for learning and his unquenchable thirst for knowledge has not been satisfied yet. These prolific encounters with the plantation were without a doubt painful and burdensome phenomenon in that it takes divinity to maintain some sanity in the insanity we live with.

In this period of reconstruction, he continues in a letter to express his painful past with the following notations:

December 14, 2005

Evening Sir,
Truly it was a phenomenal experience for me to have lived on the cutting edge of reconstruction on a plantation.

Plantation- The act of planting or setting in the earth of planting or setting in the earth for growth; the place planted; a small wood; a grove; in the Southern states, a large estate cultivated chiefly by share croppers.

Planter- One who plants, sets, introduces, or establishes; one who owns a plantation.

The word plantation signifies mistreatment, abuse, injustice etc.

To me as a boy raised on a plantation, subjected to the wishes and commands of the master or the owner of the plantation was in many instances the same as slavery.

Grandmother and I never received any compensation for our labor other than what we could eat and many times that was scarce. Often I returned home from school to find no food. Grandmother would try to put together something for me to eat and many times it consisted of peaches, blackberries and cornbread, meat was a luxury.

I was the man in the house at 7 years old I fed the hogs, milked the cows and cut the wood. At the age of 11 I drove the tractor-trailer by the day for the owner of the plantation who's name was Mr. Dave Moore. Not only did I drive 12 hours in the day, I also drove at night Mr. Moore saw to it by putting lights on the tractor.

There were many afflictions that I had to encounter for instance frost bitten feet, dew possession from the cow stepping on top of my feet and cutting it and busted blood vessels in my hand after a log wedged my hand against the wagon wheels and I could not relieve it with natural strength, so I prayed for the Lord to give me the strength and power to lift the log and He did just that.

Mr. Dave Moore would allow me to go to school half a day and work the other half a day. I would go to school in the day and work at night or work at night and go to school in the day and that went on all the way through my high school years. I graduated the head of my class. Upon finishing high school at the time of harvest I decided I had enough and I left the plantation to venture out on my own.

Now you finish the rest!! (ha-ha)

Yours in Divine Love
Dr. William H. Murphy Sr.,

The fueling factor behind his walk of faith is in the fact that the plantation experience became a transformative agent in his life by taking his negative situations and experiences to become fuel for his future. This is the power of the black Baptist church's message, in that if received in the power of the revelation of the Gospel, it will empower the receptor to rise up above the negative entanglements of life and become successful in all the endeavors he or she may meet. This power of the Gospel message has taken William Henry as a precious olive and produced oil for the lamp of life, oil for the perfuming of life, and oil for the anointing of life. Life is birthed through crushing. Interview the olive and he would share his testimony with you like this: The process of becoming a productive agent in life starts with a seed. A seed is to be planted sometimes in the uncertainty of the soil. The relationship is one of no way out. For if, the seed is to become an olive tree, the soil is unavoidable. The soil is dark and unpredictable. The germination of seed and soil is a relationship that has to be cultivated through a process called, time. Time will produce something from the seed. Time will bring forth the fruit of the labor of toiling the soil for proper nutrient balance. The sunshine is very important for growth and ripening, it will aid in the development of life. These elements help to strengthen the sweetness of the fruit. The tree has to weather the storm in order to produce good fruit, but that's not all. There is the time left on the branch and then the picking of the olive fruit. Once the fruit is picked, there is another process that the olive must go through in order to become precious oil. This process is called the olive press, where the olives are crushed and squeezed of its oil from the inside out. This is a very painful undertaking to endure, but the reward is to see the good it does for everybody else the oil comes in contact with.This oil for life, comes by the crushing of the plantation upon this olive. William Henry was crushed to produce life in the power of the Holy Spirit of Almighty God. He has been used as oil in the lives of all the people he has met. As painful as the plantation experience was upon this young man, it was what was needed to mold his character to handle all he had to endure in life. Once the soul has been set on fire by such tremendous experiences, life is fueled with a relentless pursuit for excellence. This pursuit contains a holy unction to liberate the soul to live enlarged by God. God has to move upon the soul of a person to ener-gize their faith to reach forward with respect to their past. William Henry exemplifies this fact of faith with the steady beat of his spirit. Graduating head of his class, he held his pride as an emblem of honor. He was determined to not only graduate, but with some dignity and some very strong pride. Pride at times can be destructive, if not properly directed, but also it can be an element for movement and progression in one's life. William Henry gains momentum in the plight in life that he must undergo. Some things are unavoidable in William Henry's life, because all the things will be working together for his good and God's glory. Reality not revealed immediately to him at the onset, but time will prove to him and his faith that when the divine mandate has slated you for his purpose to be fulfilled, he will not cease to be until God has been satisfied with his service. It is true that God has a time set for all people, and yet with his Omniscience, he still meshes humanity into the equation. How awesome is his infinite wisdom.

This fuel to be the head of the class was to say with clarity, that William Henry was not going to pick cotton or be somebody's "boy." He remembers day in and day out the painful reality that faced him at home and the mistreatment he and his grandmother received at the hands of the plantation owners. Studying was painful and enduring. Being hungry for both food and knowledge, he went to bed with his stomach empty but his mind and head full. He knew what it was like to eat a meal and not have the pleasure of meat. But with the meat of knowledge and the hunger for success burning in his soul, William Henry would stay up at night to feed his mind. It is the mind that will keep a man sharp and keen to the vicissitudes of life and the senses enlighten to the wave of the times. The mind muscles have to be continually developed in order to grow and become flexible so that it will not rust out or wear out. The mindset of William Henry is that while his humble and obscure beginnings were from the plantation, he is still no man's "boy" and that with the power of God and the power of self-will, where a person comes from will be the determining factor of how they choose to live in the future. He shares in his life of how we can take life by the horns and transform that beginning into becoming a powerful and productive life. Life to William Henry is the essence of being. Paul Tillich writes in his classic on the "being" says this, "Courage is self-affirmation "in-spite-of" that is in spite of that which tends to prevent the self from affirming itself." Tillich continues with this," Courage is the readiness to take upon oneself negatives, anticipated by fear, for the sake of a fuller positivity." Life is to be lived with respect to God and the preciousness of the creations he has designed with his mighty hand. The Plantation experience is a part of this man's history that solidifies the truth and the reality of the effects that slavery and its residue can have upon the life of a people who allow the residue to remain in their mind, spirit and consciousness. To stand tall in the midst of such obstacles is to say that no weapon formed or created will be able to prosper. Life offers to all of us the choices, in order to fulfill the divine mandate set by the Almighty's agenda. God navigates the circumstances of life to pilot our pilgrimage in order that we might reach that peaceful shore. The question is not if God will activate in our lives, but the issue is when God activates in our lives, how we will respond to his request for us to totally follow his leadings. William Henry demonstrates that kind of rare faith and trust that is so hard to find in this time of this writing. To be strong in the Lord is not just a catch verse to be pious or arrogant, but William Henry expresses this reality in the walk of faith that causes him to triumph. Triumphant in life is very vital to the spirit and soul, because the inner being of William Henry has within its chemistry, the steady beat of a promise of faith to his dear grandmother, to make something good out of himself. It is not what a person is driving but rather, what is it on the inside driving them through, over, and around all the obstacles that confronts them. Moreover, the beat gains momentum!

Chapter 2.

Grandma

In the childhood of William Henry, there served for him in the cultivating of continuity of character was his grandmother, Mrs. Rena Hunter. The value system that was to be instilled, in his life would come from a woman whose faith in God, would with no doubt be transferred to the bosom of her grandson. Just like Timothy of the biblical text, the companion of the Apostle Paul. The Apostle Paul shares with Timothy these words of encouragement in Second Timothy, chapter one and verses five through seven, " When I call into remembrance the unfeigned faith that is in thee, which dwelt first in thy grandmother Lois, and thy mother Eunice; and I am persuaded that in thee also. Wherefore, I put thee in remembrance that thou stir up the gift of God, which is in thee by the putting on of my hands. For God has not given us the spirit of fear; but of power, and of love, and of a strong mind."

Now at this point, much is in saying that there is a key element to the raising of children in the fear and reference of God. It is that if we are to give our children or grandchildren anything of real substance, it has to be that we must give them a God consciousness of sure footing that will keep them in the slippery places that life will bring their way. For without

35

this sure footing, William Henry would not be. William Henry is by no means perfect in his life, nor is he flawless, but without a doubt, he is faithful. It is this faithfulness; he exhibits what was demonstrated in his early childhood. In the tradition of the black Church, much is learned through observation or "caught." Listen as he now shares with us the person of his Grandmother, Mrs. Rena Hunter.

"Mrs. Rena Hunter was a very deeply religious lady. As I can remember, I was never really privileged to attend church from infancy to about seven years old. All I can remember was staying from Aunt Leana to Aunt Jennie, and to Aunt Maggie's house. I believed I stayed at Aunt Maggie's the longest for she herself had five children of her own, and of course I enjoyed the fun times I shared with my cousins, for they were the only brothers and sisters I had to play with. Aunt Maggie's oldest son, Eugene who was two years older than I was which I looked upon him as my big brother. I was staying at Aunt Maggie's when she told me that she had to take me to Millington where my mother was and that Mrs. Rena, my grandmother could pick me up and there with her would I live with. As I recall, what a sad day that was for me at seven years old, being "tossed from pillow to post." Well, it was a Saturday afternoon, when a tall black gentleman, named Charlie Hunter rode up to my mothers little hut on an old mule with a burlap bag for a saddle to pick me up and carry me to my grandmother's house. I did not want to go with that strange man, seeing that I did not know him or where I was going, but I said "Goodbye to Mama" and we rode off to grandmother's. Jolted up and down on the back of that old mule, which was across a twelve-mile bumpy road to Millington, rubbed blisters on my back-hind part until that I could not sit comfortably for days. As we arrived to grandmother's, you could see her in the near horizon, looking forward to the arrival of her grandson, she was postured there in front of her one side of a four way duplex, which had one room, a half kitchen, which she shared with Uncle Roosevelt, her elder son. Upon my arrival, I became a man at the tender age of seven years old. It was not until after, I was a full grown man and with a retrospective look back at that time of my life that I realized that grandmother only wanted me there, to carry out the chores, which constituted having a man child around the house. It was about milking the cows, feeding the hogs, cutting the wood, lighting the stove, and ect. As it relates to the religious conviction of Grandma Rena being a religious person, I think her Christological centering did not come from book learning, but through the life experiences, she endured. It was at this time, as I recall was my first time ever going to church was with my grandmother. At this time in her life, she is in her late 60s and had been through a many of storms in her life, which had fermented her faith in God and in His might and power to see her through tough and trying times. The year at this time is 1935, and at this time, brethren, you would not want to live in the south around the Tennessee valley, on the very cutting edge of Reconstruction. I believe in most instances that following Reconstruction was a lot worse than that of the most brutalism of slavery itself. Nevertheless, with the strong conviction of grandmother's faith in the power of Almighty God and her keen sense of spiritual perception, she had a sure way of getting along with white folks and getting them to favor her. It was not just her faith alone that blessed her, but it was also her strong belief system in the power of prayer. She would not lie down at night nor rise in the morning without getting on her knees to pray to God and me the same. She literally taught me how to pray. She taught one the "Lord's prayer" and carried me through that so much that finally one night as we were beginning to pray I told her, "Grandma, I can say my own prayers by myself" and she responded, "Let me hear you." Because, she had to be sure that I would thoroughly be able to say the Lord's Prayer to the letter, her faith and prayer life kept her faithful in church attendance. She was not ever going to intentionally, miss second and fourth Sunday services, and as an usher for more than seventy years of her life, she was going to have that white ushers dress kept, cleaned, white, and ready to be worn on each of her Sundays to usher. When grandma went to heaven, at age eighty-five years old, she was still and active usher on the usher's board. Grandma was truly and instrument in the Lord's hand having to mold me into the vessel as a man of God that he intended me to be. I shall always remember that it was one hot August summer in 1941, at age twelve, we were chopping cotton, Grandma said to me, "You know you are twelve years old now, revival has started, so it's time for you to sit on the mourner's bench. So that evening we left the field a little earlier than usual, so that we could get ready for church that evening and be on time. Grandma made sure that I was going to get to know God for myself. She not only made sure we went to revival, but she insisted that I sit on the mourner's bench. This was the first Tuesday evening in August of 1941 that I accepted the Lord Jesus Christ as my personal Savior. How ironic is this, I was born on a Tuesday, I was saved or converted on a Tuesday, I was called to preach the Gospel on a Tuesday as well. Praise God. So really, I am a living extension of grandmother's devotion and commitment to God. Amen."

Here we read of this phenomenal upbringing, of how vital it is for faith in God, to become in the lives of African American children and all children of Christianity. Although, William Henry does not have the fortune of having been raised in the home with both of his parents, yet he receives something greater, that is he gets introduced to real faith in God, demonstrated in the life of his grandmother. Not only is he blessed, but also he is catapulted into real life responsibility as a child, which focused his attention to recognizing the activity of God in his life. At grandmother's was the pain of the plantation, but at grandmother's was also the presence of the divine encounter with the God who holds the world in his hands. At grandmother's was the presence of an uncle who was not a responsible man, but at grandmother's was the making and the molding of a man, William Henry. At grandmother's there was the unfairness of the plantation owner, but at grandmother's there was the provisions of faith, prayer, and a trust in the power of God, to keep them safe in his arms. At grandmother's there the heat of the fields, but there was also the soothing of love and divine care provided by God through the heart of grandma. At grandmothers, there was the absence of the conveniences of life, but there was the comfort of knowing that all things work together for the good of them who love the Lord and who are the called according to his purpose. This is the work of God in the navigation of life. When God is sensed in our lives, we will realize that he is behind the scenes directing life, to introduce himself fully to us, in order for us to see him clearly working on our behalf. It is His good pleasure to see us live life in the fullness of the knowledge of him. It does not matter the age of introduction, but it does matter the acceptance of that introduction, no matter the age. William Henry help us see the importance of God being in our lives from our early years and that it is true love when family takes the responsibility of bringing one into a right relationship with God. The whole, human family that is.

To enlarge wider on this aspect, what grew out of the life of William Henry's plantation experience and decades of life, was influenced by Booker T. Washington's concept of a compromise between the South, the North, and the Negro. "Naturally, the Negroes resented at first, bitterly, signs of compromise, which surrounded their civil and political rights, even through there was to be exchanged for larger chances for economic development. Mr. Washington's programme practically accepts the alleged inferiority of the Negro race. Again in our own land, the reaction from the sentiment of which time has given to race prejudice against Negroes, and Mr. Washington withdraws many of the high demands of Negroes as men and American citizens. In other periods of intensified prejudices, the Negroe's entire tendency to self-assertion has been called forth, at this period; a policy of submission is advocated. In the history of nearly all other races and people, the doctrine preached at such crisis has been mainly self-respect is worth more than lands and houses, and that a people who voluntarily surrender such respect, or cease striving for it, are not worth more civilizing. In answer to this, it had been claimed that the Negro could survive only through submission. Mr. Washington has distinctly asked Black people to give up at least, for the present three things:

First- Political Power, Second – Insistence on Civil Rights, and Third - Higher Education of Negro Youth, and concentrate all their energies on industrial education, the accumulation of wealth and the Conciliation of the South. This policy has been courageously and insistently been advocated for over fifteen years, and has been triumphant for perhaps ten years. As a result of this tender of palm branch, what has been the return? In the years, there have accrued:

(1) The disfranchisement of the Negro
(2) The legal creation of a distinct status of civil inferiority for the Negro
(3) The steady withdrawal of aid from institutions for the higher training of the Negro. (Dubois Writings, pgs.398-399)

These movements are not, to be sure, direct results of Mr. Washington's teachings; but his propaganda has without any doubt, helped their speedier accomplishment. This was the era of the upbringing of Dr. William H. Murphy, Sr. Amen

I'm Determined To Be Somebody, Someday
(The Resolution of The Negro Youth)
By William Herbert Brewster

The present conditions and dark circumstances,
May make it appear that 1 have not a chance;
The odds may be against me, this fact I admit,
I haven't much to boast of—just a little faith and
  grit;
In spite of the things that stand in my way,
**I'M DETERMINED TO BE SOMEBODY,
SOMEDAY,**

There's no royal blood a-coursing in my veins,
No great family background for me remains;
I haven't had a chance as others have had,
My Irving conditions have been kind-a bad;
But, it makes no difference what folks think or say,
**I'M DETERMINED TO BE SOMEBODY,
SOMEDAY!**

Some may think that I have made a poor start,
Well, maybe I have; but I'll handle that part;
At the end of each round, I'll be on my feet,
For there's something in ME, that's hard to beat;
The fight may be tough, but I'M IN IT to stay,
**For, I'M DETERMINED TO BE SOMEBODY,
SOMEDAY!**

There's really somewhere I would like to go,
There's truly, some things that I would like to
  know;
There're, certainly, some things that I'd like to see,
And, something SPECIAL I'd like to be;
Let others do as they will or may,

41

But, as for ME, **I'VE JUST GOT TO BE SOMEBODY, SOMEDAY!**

As a member of a once down trodden race, To the courts of Heaven, I've appealed my case; I know, that Jehovah is (he Judge on the bench, Thou, men may deride, and lynch;
My blood will cry from the ground and say.
"Tho' you slay me, **I'll BE SOMEBODY SOMEDAY!**"

My head may be bloody, and my skin may be black,
But NOTHING shall throw me off the track;
I'll climb the ladder, round by round
Until my feet strike higher ground;
And when I do, just remember what I say,

I'M DETERMINED TO BE SOMEBODY, SOMEDAY.

Chapter 3.

Divine Calling and Assignment

O ne of the most critical things, which Pastor Murphy shared with all of the sons of the church, was to make sure that we were sure we had received a "divine encounter" from the Lord. For it was highly stressed that it was the "divine encounter" which was going to be able to keep us on the battlefield for the Lord. Without that divine encounter, Satan would definitely win the battle and the victory over your ministry. Dr. Cleophus J. LaRue, Associate Professor of Homiletics at Princeton Theological Seminary shares in his book, *"The Heart of Black Preaching"* a question that is asked in the theological circles about the dynamic of "black preaching" says, " That the reason for the distinctive power of black preaching lies deeper, resting finally in the soul of black Christian experience, that is, in the way that African Americans have come, in the refining fires of history, to understand the character of God and the ways God works through scripture and sermon in their lives today... In essence, the distinctive power of black preaching is a matter, not merely of special techniques but of extraordinary expe- riences that have among other results, forged a unique way of understanding the Bible and applying those insights in very practical ways." Dr. LaRue's perspective helps to bring more clarity of the unique characteristics that the art of black preaching offers to Christianity in general and specific. However, we hold dear that the black Baptist church has set itself in the seat of forerunner as it reflects the peculiar power of the preacher to expound on the Word of God. Although we are not at all suggesting that the black Baptist church stands alone with its preachers, but we are giving them their due respect and reverence to the fact that this truth, should no longer be overlooked or underestimated. God has placed a rare anointing upon the black Baptist church and her preachers that is like none other. Historically we can find that one of the black Baptist churches as Dr. Henry Mitchell, *"Black preaching: The Recovery of a Powerful Art"*, points out "greatest evidence of the power of Black preaching is that the Black belief system of folk Christianity has kept its believers alive and coping-even when in an oppressed condition that would have crushed many."

Divine Calling "An Assignment." Dr. Murphy shares with us his divine encounter:

"How mystical of course and phenomenal it was, how God ushered me into the earth realm being born of a young woman at the age of fourteen whose mother and father died when she was nine years old. They died during the epidemic of influenza in 1917 leaving my mother and her sister to live with her father's elder sister, Aunt Lena. And when Aunt Lena discovered that momma was with child at age fourteen she put her out with no place to go. Ended up she did at her other aunt's house; Aunt Jennie who blesses the Lord was also a midwife and served to bring me into the world."

"Now imagine a fourteen-year-old girl with child, no education, no experience, no mother and no father. How she kept me until I was seven years old is amazing. Oh how I remember going from pillow to post just anywhere she could drop me to get me off her hands. Finally, at age seven, grandmother, my daddy's mother took me. Oh my, oh my.

What an honorable experience it was. In spite of the hardship I encountered I truly loved my mother. I cried many, many nights and days to not only be with my mother, but also just to see her. Oh dear readers, truly our God works in mysterious ways, his wonders...to perform. He still plants his footsteps upon the seas and rise in every star."

In the book written by Dr. William H. Myers entitled, "The Irresistible Urge To Preach", he records the call to preach stories of African American preachers from across the nation and shares with us his interpretation of the "Call to preach" narrative. He says, "That a divine call to preach is described as an internal urge ....for too long the experiential encounter with the divine has been looked upon with a jaundiced eye, simply because we never know everything about that intensely personal moment." Dr. Myers continues with this, "The examination of the content of the stories reveals that the call to preach can be understood as a process, a "rite to passage." Six stages of call are identified: early religious exposure, experience, struggle, search, sanction, and surrender."

Murphy continues: "Truly my destiny was in his hands, indeed one of the best things that could have ever happened to me was that momma could not keep me and therefore gave me to my grandmother. My, what a blessing the hardship, the loneliness, and suffering that I encountered were well worth the many benefits I received. Such as faith in God, discipline, the knowledge and value of self worth, the importance of achieving excellence, respect for my elders, table manners, ethics and possession of common sense. Known in the olden days as Mother Wit or wisdom from God. Being able to see what needs to be done and doing it. "Praise the Lord." I remember one Saturday evening I had the yearning to see my mother so I asked grandmother to give me thirty-five cents to catch the bus from Lucy, TN to Millington, TN where momma lived. Grandmother refused to give me the thirty-five cents and I thought that was terrible."

We see that young William Henry struggles with the internal paternal connectiveness that holds dear to his young heart. He walks with the uncertainty of the times wanting so dearly to rest again to rest upon the bosom of his mother, that he now is dealing with the tough choice of making a decision, that may change the course of his life. At times, we have watched Pastor Murphy make some tough choices in his faith walk. So many times, he has said yes and no at critical venues that even those of us whom walk so closely with him, thought that maybe he was not aware of the impact that those decisions, would have upon the lives he had so much influence in. Now we see that sometimes when God speaks we must trust by faith that in the time to come, it will be revealed, to us that God has a better plan for our lives and a bigger perspective for our journey in life. Faith walking is a very rewarding life and yet it can birth some doubt into those to whom you are leading if their faith has not fully matured.

"That Spring, I had worked so hard trying to pick the cotton, corn, etc. and the gardens, my goodness gracious we were right in the middle of picking cotton. It was in late September and I felt that I deserved as much, but grand-mother refused. I really think grandmother had a feeling, an unction that I would not return. She knew that I was tired. After all, we never were paid for anything anyway. Only when we worked out by the day, but nothing from our boss, the plantation owner. He always said that we had borrowed or used the earnings on food and supplies. I remember the year before we had made five bails of cotton and I just knew we had some monies coming that year. Just before Christmas, it was and my expectation of Christmas was so high and I wanted and waited with much anticipation on grandmother to return from the big house. Finally, I looked down the road and saw grandmother coming. I could see that she was crying. I ran out to meet her wondering what in the world was wrong. I questioned her and she replied, "Mr. Moore said we don't have anything coming again this year." She went to explain the reason he gave for not paying us any earnings. Nevertheless, I continued the next year, but now I wanted to see momma and grandmother would not give me the bus fare. Goodness, gracious I was determined to see my mother so I dressed for the occasion, packed my little bag of clothes, and walked twelve miles to Millington, TN to see momma. When I arrived at momma's house, I told momma what I had done. She left the decision to me as to whether or not I would return to the plantation. In the early part of the week grandmother came for me I knew she would but of course she claimed ownership for as she said to my mother "this is my boy, I raised him." However, momma left the decision to me. I suppose my tenure with grandmother had ended. The teaching and training I needed had been accomplished. God was moving upon me on to explore other things. "Bless his holy name." I really had no inkling about my divine calling or anointing to preach the gospel. I was eighteen years old. There were those of course who envisioned or had revelations concerning my calling, but not me. They could see the anointing upon me. My Aunt Lena use to call me "Preacher" when I was just a baby even then she could see something unusual about me. I remember when my wife Ella and I was engaged she was anxious for me to see and meet her Godmother. So one Sunday afternoon, I decided to accommodate her, so we went down the street to her godmother's house, walked up on the porch, and knocked on the door. When the door opened, her godmother came, and she looked at my wife and me and said, "Momma Jones, Momma Jones this is my boyfriend and then Momma Jones looked at me and said "my goodness, boy you are a preacher" and I readily replied "No Ma'am I ain't no preacher." As she turned to go back in the house, her response was "You may not know it but you are." Listen to his keen recall ability of the events that surrounded his development as a man of promise and possibility. The mystical point of these events is that many times it can be noted that others can see the evidence or aura of something divine being manifested in our person-hood, long before we can see it or realize that its something there. God has a unique way of manifesting the divine to us through the testimony of others while shadowing us with his presence.

He continues: "That was in the month of September 1949, four years later the second Tuesday in August 1953; I was employed by, The American Snuff Company. While resting and hiding from my boss, sitting in a chair in what was called the boiler room, watching to see if my boss would approach the door. I could see him before he could see me through the door because the door was made somewhat, horizontally. Before he would come to the door to open it, I would get up and pretend to be busy. Oh, my Lord of course, all of a sudden God said to me in a tone of voice I had never heard before, "Go and preach my word." I attempted to get up and run but I could not move I became paralyzed from my head to my feet and blind that I could not see. It was as if a black sheet was put over me and covered me wholly. So, I could not see. All I could do was just sit there until the Lord finished anointing me. So that is the thick darkness passed from me and I could see. Then I jumped and ran out of the room. I went to my boss and told him what had happened to me, then he began to with his prejudiced self make fun of me with his, yeahing, and mocking, indeed, he did." One of the most difficult things to do as its related to the divine being operative in one's life, is that the fact of sharing that activity with those whom have no inkling as to what you are talking about. When God moves upon the heart of a person or persons, they too filled, with a certain sense of uncertainty and awe. God is infinite in being and it can be mind blowing to have these kinds of encounters experienced through and by the finite. This is why Pastor Murphy has always insisted on all preachers, both sons and daughters, to be sure that it was a "God calling" and not a "self calling." A God calling would fuel and refuel one's conviction during tough times, but a self- calling would fade and fatigue under the pressures of life's heavy load. During the process of transformation, God calls and beckons the spirit to respond in such a way, even those of your family and peers become infused with a sense of curiosity as to what the "calling" is to produce in one's life. Transformation takes time to produce the ripened fruit for the work that God has purposed in one's life.

He continues: "As God would have it that evening as I left work on my way home, I got on the streetcar bus and low and behold Reverend Douglas Malone was on the bus and there was only one seat left on the bus and that was beside him. As I sat down and greeted him, I began to tell him what had happened to me. He listened attentively and his response was, "I'm sure you were called to preach the gospel of Jesus Christ, but I tell you what, I tell you what to do, you go home and get on your knees and ask God if he has called you to preach and if so, reveal it to you thoroughly because man you don't want to make a mistake, for preaching the gospel is serious business." Now this juggles the memories, in that Pastor Murphy relived these instructions he received, I believe, in the lives of all to whom he heard that God had called to preach under his tutelage. Living with the reality to preach the gospel is very burdensome at times. In the life of his ministry, I say without reservation, that there has not been to my knowledge, any other son or daughter to whom much doubt was given to the authenticity of a divine calling than that of the author. In recollection of those tender moments, it took a total of three years to get an opportunity to share a trial sermon with the open congregation. For it was not that

Pastor Murphy did not believe that the calling was not sure, but he wanted to make sure that I was sure because he had at that time, recently endure the embarrassment of those whom had great trial sermons and testimonies of a divine calling, but they return to deny the call. This became very frustrating for Pastor Murphy in that he loves people and he has never tried to stand intentionally in the way of any man or woman whom felt that God had spoken to their heart. It is this kind of human love and devotion to ministry that has given him much heartache and personal disappointment with persons whom he has afforded much love and generosity to. He has taken the ministry of the Gospel of Jesus Christ to his heart as his divine mandate to do all that he can to become pleasing in God's eyesight and to the betterment of his fellow man or woman. Listen closely as he continues to unfold his bosom:

"Well, I took him at his word when I arrived at home my wife and I had very little to say to each other. I tried to eat my supper, but had no appetite so I just sat around watching and wondering what to say to God, I even watched the "Late, Late Show." Finally, I decided to go to bed, but I had to get on my knees, so I did and I prayed, "Lord if you have called me to preach, please reveal it to me thoroughly because I don't want to make a mistake." Then I rose from my knees and got in the bed with the intentions of going to sleep "Hallelujah" but could not, all I could do was preach. I couldn't even control my own voice or mind. All I could do was preach non-stop until I was wringing wet with sweat. I finally, "hallelujah" figured the only way I could stop preaching was to tell God I was satisfied that he had called me to preach and that I would do his will. Only one thing I said to the Lord "Please make me a good preacher. I do not want to be a Jack Leg preacher," (according to my concept of what a Jack Leg Preacher was). I got off the bed, rather got out of the bed, got down on my knees and said to the Lord "I am satisfied you have called me to preach the gospel of Jesus Christ and I will do your will but please let me go to sleep because, I got to go to work in the morning." I got off my knees got back in the bed and went right on to sleep, "Praise God."

One of the most critical things that Pastor Murphy has ever shared his concern about with all of the preachers at Greater Ebenezer was this notion of being a "jack-legged preacher." He detested that idea of a lazy and uneducated or unread preacher. He insisted that we all would keep ourselves, well read at all times. Reading was and still is his regular agenda even today. He has never allowed the excuse of not having enough to do as an outlet of not being able to hear a word from the Lord. He would inform us that God was always speaking to us through various resources available to those whom kept reading. Read, read, read, read, and read! Read everything, because God may say a word in your reading to fuel your faith and give revelation to your dream. Many times, we preachers did not understand his passion for reading, because many not until this writing, even knew anything about his upbringing, so we never understood why he was and still is so serious about reading. It still bothers him deeply that many who were so talented and gifted in the Lord were so complacent about reading the books he recommended and their lack of desire for furthering their theological education. One of the most serious students of Pastor Murphy is none other than, Elder Jeanetta Parks. Elder Parks undoubtedly has the passion for reading and information as a scholar in her own right. She was at the forefront to the foundations of learning at the Greater Ebenezer School of Theological Learning, whereas she kept the edge on the newest and latest of books and resources. Many times as a young man, I would visit her office and her home, and without surprise, you could notice many books opened to pages, some highlighted as well as pages bent or marked, for she was always in hot pursuit for new revelation. We share a unique connection, in that we both preached our trial sermons together on August 31, 1986 and were both licensed to preach on that same evening. Elder Parks was ordained in September 1989. She is perhaps one of the most biblically educated women from Pastor Murphy's ministry. Although there are many others, she still stands tall amongst them all. Her service and sacrifices for many years is unparallel to any other sister in ministry that we have witnessed at Greater Ebenezer. She is well seasoned in the Word of the Lord and her ministry is a personified example of the diversity of her "Father" in the ministry's innovative and liberal perspective to the totality of ministry within the black Baptist church. She followed many other sisters' footsteps, but she surpasses many because of her undaunted following. The black Baptist church has produced another diamond!

Pastor Murphy holds dear to his heart education, primarily biblical education. Many would consider him as one who has a relentless pursuit for theological education excellence. Dr. Cornel West, in his book, *"Prophesy Deliverance: An Afro-American Revolutionary Christianity,"* says that " black people became Christians for intellectual, existential, and political reasons.....the African slaves' search for identity could find historical purpose in the exodus of Israel out of slavery and personal meaning in the bold identification of Jesus Christ with the lowly and downtrodden. Christianity also is first and foremost a theodicy, a triumphant account of good over evil" His total conviction is that, one must have a balance of learning, a burning, and a yearning. The learning is for the head. The head is for wisdom and knowledge. The head must become filled with information to cultivate, the inspiration that God will give. Many people are full with inspiration, but not earned information, so therefore there is no true illumination for their revelation. In order to acquire information, there has to be the sacrifice made for the seeking of such information. Time spent in the late night oil burning to satisfy the thirst for the knowledge a preacher needs exposure to; is without a doubt a priceless jewel. Therefore, without it, the church has to endure the miseducation about our salvation in our celebrations. The burning is for the spirit. The spirit must be set aflame with the conviction that God has spoke and touched the being in the inner self with his mandate upon their soul. The voice of God, must be distinctively heard and adhered to, in order for one's life to have direction and destiny. The yearning is for excellence in one's life with the undeniable thrust and pursuit to do all one can for God and humanity. Helping people and being in touch with the realities that affect their lives is necessary for their survival and our meaning in life. God has placed us in the lives of each other in order to bring some harmony to their lives and some melody to ours by orchestrating the circumstances of life. He can bring music to our lives as we share intercourse with the actions and activities that affect us all together. God gives us understanding in our pursuits that are engaged in productive discourse. He directs our lives in such a unique way, that at many junctures, bequeathed we are, into the presence of his divine nature. The prophet of the Old Testament, Isaiah 6:1b, puts it this way, "I saw also the Lord sitting upon a throne, high and lifted up, and his trained filled the temple."

William Murphy continues:

"Thursday evening of that week, which was the second week of August of 1953, I went to Choir Rehearsal and I thought it a good opportunity to inform my Pastor of my divine experience, which is the "calling" to preach. Not withstanding Pastor Slay had just asked me the week before to serve on the Deacon Board. I told him I would think about it and let him know. Not that I had any reservations; no, no certainly not. I just wanted to gloat over the idea with my kinfolk. After all, it was not everyday young men are asked to serve in such prestigious position on the Board of Deacons of our church. I went to our Pastor's office and broke to him the news telling him of my experience. He listened patiently then said to me "I'm not surprised, I knew it already" and shared with me this advice, "You will have to be careful, you are a nice looking young man, and you dress nice. The girls are going to be after you and they can ruin you. So be wise and discreet." Of course, I thanked him humbly for I really loved and respected my pastor.

"Praise God."

The advice he received from Pastor Slay was without a doubt a timeless treasure. Within that piece of advice is the wise counsel, to which plenty of young, gifted, and articulate black preachers could have well used for the vices that snared their ministries and their growth potential. Halted are many preachers in their pursuits for excellence, because of the seduction of the lust of the flesh, the lust of the eyes and the pride of life. These three destructive dynamics are always the lowest common denominator so prevalent in the lives of so many ministries becoming lamed and handicapped, that it has become an epidemic in proportion to the successful comparisons.

William Henry continues: "Well, my goodness gracious, that coming Sunday morning August 1953, I was sitting in the choir stand and Pastor Slay turned and looked back at me from his big chair. "Brother Murphy I want you to preach your trial sermon tonight." Oh my goodness I almost fainted, but I could not refuse so I said, "yes sir." My wife who sang soprano asked me "What did Pastor say?" I replied, "He said that I am to preach my trial sermon tonight." Her quick reply was, "You can not preach no trial sermon, and you are not ready." But to me ready or not ready, I was going to try." Fortunately, I had been studying with Reverend Douglas Malone, getting some pointers from him and he and I had been working on my trial sermon. Yeah, just incase whenever

Pastor would ask I would be ready. So we had decided on the text, St. John 5:1-9. The subject was "Helping Humanity."

"My, my, my how the word got around so quickly that evening. I do not know but look like every body and their brother were there. The church was well packed, it only seated about six hundred people, but even the little balcony was full and did we have a time in the Lord. The Holy Spirit sanctioned my calling in a mighty, mighty way. Therefore, I thought I was going to do that every time I preached. Boy! was I in a for a great surprise. Truly, I failed a many, many, many times afterwards. "Praise God." Because, it was in my failures that awakened me to the knowledge of my needs. Indeed it did. I needed a religious education. That is when I went to my Daddy and told him I wanted to enroll in S.C. Owens College. My daddy was so inspired, to know that his son was going to college, that he paid my first tuition. How I wanted to enroll in every class possible and take every subject I possibly could."

Failure can be a tool that God can use to our benefit and to his glory. Failure, for William Henry was without a notion, a tool to fuel his desire to learn everything possible. He well demonstrated that knowledge was power. He is a prime example of what is meant by Dr. Na'im Akbar, in his landmark book, *"Breaking the Chains of Psychological Slavery"*, he suggests this, "that in order to break these chains of psychological slavery, one must understand that slavery was not necessarily a physical thing or condition, but it was also a mental bondage, slapped upon the psyche' of those who were to be enslaved from the mind out, they in turn would become imprisoned by the loss of conscious-ness (awareness) of themselves." William Henry survived the mindset from the plantation because he well understood that in order to be free from the impact that the plantation would or could have upon his mind, being always aware of what God had called him to do, that with education being his only option, he would transform William Henry into the giant of faith he has become. William Henry survived the racism that was so rapidly growing in the region of the country of his up bringing, that it is amazing that he is so calm in his personhood. With the rage that could have catapulted him in many directions, he consciously focused his agenda in the direction of the calling upon his heart that he felt probing and pricking his spirit to follow. Walking into the unknown can be frightening to those who are weak at heart, but for William Henry, the tougher the challenge, the more tenacity he would display. The darker the path, the more faith he would exhibit. The greater the difficulty, the deeper the commitment he would demonstrate. William Henry is rare in his footsteps because he has seen a plenty of his peers, who have fallen by the wayside into drugs, alcoholism, mental breakdowns, prison, and even death. He has been truly highly favored of God.

Chapter 4.

First Baptist and Brown's Creek "1958"

First Baptist Church

One of the most exciting times in the life of a preacher, besides his called to preach encounter, is his first church as Pastor. William Henry has now emerged from those humbling days of the plantation to these moments of grace that he is now embarking upon. He is filled with the expectancy of greatness. His hope has lifted his burden. He is no longer trying to outlive the past, but now he has been catapulted to the front seat of the train, seeking to reach that peaceful shore of glory. He is faced with his divine encounter manifesting itself and materializing before his humble eyes. This really does not need any commentary. We just want him to flow, listen. "My first assignment as pastor came in a mysterious way, it was truly a miraculous occurrence. The Lord did it that way for sure. I thought I was ready for the office of pastor from "jump-street" and as a result, I was in for many disappointments, because I was not all I thought I was. Although I was privileged to preach almost every Sunday, for no sooner than I preached my trial sermon, Pastor Slay made

me his number one or first assistant at Chapel, for he said,"
This boy has his head on straight." I would be at Hills Chapel
on first and third Sunday, and Ebenezer was a second and
fourth Sunday. Pastor Slay was a very liberal minded person he
loved to share, and did not mind sharing his pulpit and of course
he could afford to being the pastor of two churches. He gave
me many opportunities, maybe because of my faithfulness and
loyalty. I shall never forget it was the week before; I was called
to preach, he had asked me to serve on the Deacon Board, which
was exceptional to ask twenty-one years old to hold such honor
and servant hood."

When leadership is destined to be the order that God
almighty has purposed within and through a person's life,
he places in the pathways individuals whom he will use to
mold us. Dr. Cornel West in his phenomenal book, *"Race
Matters"* says this as it pertains to leadership, *"Quality
leadership is neither the product of one great individual nor
the result of odd historical accident. Rather, it comes from
deeply bred traditions and communities that shape and mold
talented gifted persons."* We thank God for the keen insight
of the late Pastor E. L. Slay, whose faithfulness to the gospel
ministry, opened the door to allow the giftedness of William
Henry to come forth. This has been the mindset of Pastor
Murphy from the time of my encounter in the 1980's until
this day. He sees the spark that is in the eyes of the preacher
to share the burden that was placed upon their spirit. He has
been a preacher's preacher and Pastor.

"Nevertheless, I suppose my punctuality and exemplary
services were proof of my worthiness for such a prestigious
office. Of course, now I served as a Sunday School Teacher
and was President of the Inspirational Choir and under my
leadership, both auxiliaries grew to its largest number ever.
The Sunday school class grew so large that Pastor Slay had to
divide my class to reduce the class size. Anyway, I had a good
rapport with my pastor. One reason was I really loved and

respected my pastor. (Hello), after being licensed and ordained Pastor Slay would even let me baptize the new members, "boy", I thought I was really something while serving as Pastor Slay's assistant I still had an overwhelming urge to pastor as an under-shepherd of a church. I just wanted to be a pastor, so every time I got an opportunity I grabbed it. I pursued pasturage at First Baptist, Millington Tennessee, was no exception. I was told that First Baptist Church where I was born, and where many of my grade school classmates were members were without a pastor. "Boy", I readily pursued an opportunity to preach there, I cannot remember the entire transaction but the mission was accomplished. I cannot remember who interceded to get me the appointment all I know is that Bro. Luther Hall, was chairman of the Deacon Board and he was in my corner. I was granted an opportunity was ready so I thought I guess looking back on the occasion I was just excited, uptight, over-zealous, and hyped-up. And did I blow-it, I failed so bad, I tell you I wanted to disappear but I hung around through out the day for the ushers union was scheduled to meet that Sunday afternoon at 3:30 pm, so I went to that service and of course there were several other preachers there that aspired to become the pastor of First Baptist. One preacher, a Rev. Hurley who preached that evening for the ushers and "did he?" He preach so that my Aunt Leana shouted, and another preacher held up his hand and proclaimed First Baptist is vacant and need a pastor and here he is, and everybody applauded. Well I felt like there goes my chance; but that same evening the choir union met back at First Baptist a six Church Union which meant that each Church's choir were privileged to sing an A and B selection and the host church was responsible for singing what was called the dedication number. There I was sitting on the side siege looking for another chance to be heard. The choir union had as its president a great woman of the Christian Community, a Mrs. Williams, who knew me when I was born and she said so. She rose to her feet in her usual graceful manner said, "We are blessed with a young man here tonight that I have known all of his life, young Rev. William Murphy we are going to ask him to sing the dedication number." (Boy oh boy) "Here I go again." I rendered a song that I had been singing with Ebenezer's choir my, my when I finished singing, and as soon as the deacon's of First Baptist could get my attention Deacon Hall beckoned for me to meet with the board, in their little office in the rear of the church. The deacons, lead by Bro. Hall, asked several questions, "First are you interested in the office of Pastor?", and of course, you know what my answer was, then they wanted to know if they call me as pastor would I please make no difference in the board members. I know that the rule according to church ordinance was that each board deacon were equal in authority and the only reason we elect a chairman is supposed to be for the convenience of the pastor, in case there is business at hand the pastor will not have to call each board member but the chairman would assist in that endeavor. Therefore, I quickly responded, "Yes, I promise" and then the deacons went immediately before the congregation and announced a called meeting to elect a pastor that coming Friday evening and so they did. I was immediately elected pastor and granted the privilege of delivering my expectance sermon the second Sunday morning in July. Amen. I arrived to be heard, the fourth Sunday of June 1954, "Boy", did I put fourth some hours in preparation for that worship experience."

"That Sunday the deacons were gathered on the lawn of the church trying to convince a preacher that they had a pastor. What happened was, the preacher was that man that preached at the ushers union and ran everybody out of the church and of had him an appointment to preach at First Baptist the next Sunday. However, when he finished preaching at the union he went home. That was a mistake, because, I stayed and sang that same evening at the choirs union. Therefore, they told him, "here comes newly elected pastor and you will have to speak with him.' I never stopped walking; I proceeded to the little office. The preacher came in behind me with a sad story, his wife was ill and he need money plus, he had no food at home and of course in that day some preachers just did so to eat. I finally told him I would think about it, in which I did as to what effect it would have on the service and me. By the time service commenced, I had made up my mind to let him preach. I remember explaining to the congregation what was happening that last Sunday the board gave reverend Hines an appointment to preach this Sunday so I am going to honor the appointment by letting him preach. I also exclaimed the fact of me being the pastor and that I will have many opportunities to preach in the future and the congregation agreed so I put him up and what a shame, what a disgrace. I really think he forgot his message, anyway the Holy Spirit disapproved of his action anyway he exclaimed and he exalted out of breath "I never do anything like this for as long as I live." Well the next Sunday, that is, the next meeting Sunday I preached my acceptance message and the battled began. The heat was intensified; the adversary was able to use many of the members to speak and do his dirty work and especially those that were unlearned or just plain old, outright, ignorant. My first encounter was in choir rehearsal, I went to rehearsal in order to teach a couple of songs that I loved and sung with my home choirs, that is Ebenezer and Hill Chapel choirs. I made a suggestion to the musician that we teach one of the songs, upon doing so one fellow who was the manager of the choir bro. James Nelson pointed his finger in my face and said in a commanding and angry tone, "you don't come out here telling us what to do." Of course, that was a big mistake for he signed his death notice. He died the next day. I preached his funeral that weekend. Well, I had just preached the superintendent of Sunday schools funeral the week before because he swore that, "that boy would never pastor me." He made that statement the night elected me as pastor. He too had signed his death notice. The word got around, 'do not mess with that young preacher, something' might happen to you.' Well it seemed like I had adopted the concepts, style, appreciations and aspirations of the city church modes for I wanted everything to be tops, I desired everything in Christian service and especially the house of the Lord. So I called a church meeting in about six months that we might consider decorating the inner courts of the sanctuary, which needed improvement so bad, the floors were just plan concrete, no tile, no pulpit, no choir stand, and the walls needed painting! I just could not stand it, the way things were looking. However, what do you know, they voted the suggestion down, their reason, 'we just got out of debt and we ain't going to get back in debt. Therefore, that was it. Coming out of an up to date church such as Ebenezer in Hills Chapel were, I was very disappoint over their actions. Nevertheless, I went on. It so happened that within a couple of weeks, the city of Millington incorporated the church into the city limit and it required that all building be brought of the code by all city pacifications so this was my chance to get something done. I called another church meeting to inform them of what the city's requirements were. The new ordinances required that we install inside restrooms, which required running water, etc. To do such required a loan from City State Bank to purchase materials etc. "What do you know," they approved me. Boy, I went to the bank and borrowed enough money to not only install restrooms but to, title the floors, build a choir-stand, pulpit, and paint the whole inside. Man-o-man, I hired me a carpenter to do the carpenter work, and I got some men to help me do the painting. I went to Memphis and found some theater chairs, which were very pretty and installed them! Oh, I had that place looking like it was really "God's house". The members would drop by and peep in admiringly. The work was completed for the Sunday service. I made sure of that, imagine all week what was done. But some of the deacons never forgave me for that trick I pulled in borrowing monies to do all that decorating. So they waited for an opportunity to get even with me. At least two followers had it bad, they just didn't like me. It seemed what ever I did regardless to its needs or whatever it was never right. So they waited until they got me to Calvary so they could crucify me. And that they did. In 1959, I had planned to attend the National Baptist Convention in San Francisco, CA, which always convened Tuesdays after Labor

Day. I knew we would have Men's day the fourth Sunday in August and there would be enough money for me to go to the Convention. So I had planned to meet with the trustee board on Monday as per usual, to disperse. When I arrived for the meeting only one trustee showed up, and he and I sat there waiting for the longest on the others to show, so finally he said, "Pastor, I don't think the other fellows are coming!" I said, "Why? He said, "Because we met early and took care of all the business." I was so angry with him for letting me sit there all of that time without saying something. Inasmuch as he knew what they had done! They had not only paid the bills but they had paid off some of the other bills just to disperse all of the money, so that there would be no money left for me to use, to bear my expense to go to the convention. "Oh my Lord, was I upset", here I am, I've made plans for Mom and I to travel with the late Dr. BT Hopkins and his wife to California for the convention and no money! I went back home that night angry, studying ways and means how I could still make the trip. I came up with the idea to go and borrow the money I needed from the People State Bank where the church had an account, all I was required to do was to get two Deacons to co-sign. Now that's going to present a problem from jump street, but I'm determined and I'm going to accomplish my objective regardless, "Hell can freeze over, "I'm going to the convention." I went to the bank and picked up the applications, and I proceeded, I went to the Deacon's chairperson, Brother Hall. Now Brother Hall was my man, my main man. He was with me through thick and thin, I remember a couple of weeks after I had been called to the pastorate I was in line at the unemployment office to get my check and lo and behold in the line there was none other than the former Pastor of First Baptist and he knew me. I had no memory of meeting him, but he said to me "aren't you Murphy the recently elected Pastor of First Baptist?" I said "Yes". He continued "Well you have some fine people there, but you'd better watch that Deacon Hall, he's a snake in the grass." I replied, "Sho' nough" and he went on and on telling me about First Baptist Church, would you believe it? I some-what listened to him and started treating Bro. Hall cool and with a long handle spoon, per say, until one afternoon I was on my way to Mama house and Bro. Hall was walking on his way home. I stopped and offered him a ride but he refused said he just wanted to walk. But he did lean over in the window of my car and said "Pastor I don't know why you treat me like you do, but that's alright your going to find out that I am one of the best friends you're ever going to have." Boy those words begin to ring and ring and ring in my head. The truth of the matter is I almost lost a good friend that is for sure! So I went to Bro. Hall to sign the papers, I than went to Bro. Swanson, I then knew upon going I would have to persuade him to sign, anyway he reluctantly signed. I did not borrow but three hundred dollars when I should have borrowed more, because when I paid a couple of bills, I really did not have enough to make the journey but we went with what we had left. Mom and I, we ran out of money before we could even get there. I saw my Pastor and he shared ten dollars with me and that's all we had to get back home on." Learning how to handle the critics is acquired through trials and trusting the integrity of peoples' intentions and their demonstrations of faithful stewardship. When people render service, the Lord is concerned about the motives of the heart. God will honor those renderings that have the unselfish intentions embedded within them. Many times as a young man, I would visit the church looking forward to the fellowship of being around my pastor, is when we would be in the midst of fixing or cleaning something at the church, that he would say, "Bud, as a preacher, you must have a certain respect and reverence for the Lord's house. We cannot handle his house like it is insignificant. No Sir, man you must keep it clean, because God honors his Holy place, and when we invite him to tabernacle with us, we want him to be proud of us." As I have visited the many churches of Pastor Murphy's ministry, there is the residue of his style of reverence for the Lord's house like none other.

He continues: "The whole trip was so miserable. The first thing, the car was too crowded, Mrs. Hopkins had too many hatboxes, and the trunk of the car was filled to capacity. Therefore, we rode with hatboxes in our laps. The Hopkins were not the kind of folks you would want to travel with anyway, with their whims made for a miserable trip to the extent I promise the Lord I would never in my whole life travel that far in someone else's car and I have not until this day and that was forty-eight years ago. Well anyway, when we returned in the next couple of weeks on a Thursday, my cousin Willie B. called me, well she really called to see if I was back from the convention and it so happened I was. She informed me by saying, "You had better come out here, and the deacons have called a meeting to turn you off as pastor." "Oh, my goodness," here we go, what am I to do now. Well I desired to go out there to the meeting and surprise them for I knew they were not expecting me. As I walked into the front doors every eye was on me, I immediately took me a seat in the rear of the sanctuary. Bro. Bill Bonds had the floor, making such statements as, "We are here to night to take care of business, you all know why we came; we came to declare the pulpit vacant. For that preacher is too big for us, we don't need a big preacher, we just need a preacher that will preach to us and teach us. Not a big preacher, running all over the country like some big shot! So let's get on with our business." He then proceeded to entertain a motion to declare the pulpit vacant. I cannot remember just who made the motion and who seconded it. However when they made the count it was sixteen "yes" and fifteen "no" therefore they declared the pulpit vacant by one vote. When that was determined, all hell broke loose. They wanted to fight Brother Will Nelson who was in my corner, through his hat off the floor and stomped it. He declared he was going to kill every nigger in the house that stood against his pastor! I immediately ran to the front and screamed out "Brothers and Sisters we are in the Lord's House we cannot do this. But this meeting was

not legal I am calling a legal meeting tomorrow evening so
dismiss yourselves and come tomorrow evening", so they
all went home. My, my, my! What a trauma! That night I
pondered the whole situation in my mind prayerfully consid-
ering what must I do? The next day I went by where Bro. Hall,
the chair, worked to perceive his actions, and it seemed he was
not concern for he said, "No one can turn you off. You are our
pastor so come on back Sunday as usual." Man oh man, "No",
I said to my brother, "It is not like we must get this straighten
out now, I cannot wait until Sunday morning and come out
here in disturbance, so tell everyone you see we are going to
meet tonight." Bro. Hall agreed, "Okay", he exclaimed, "We
will meet tonight." I then went home back to Memphis, to wait
that evening for the meeting. Well it was about five o'clock
in the evening, it started raining as if it would never stop, to
the extent I said to Mama, "Honey I guess the Lord doesn't
want me to pastor that church." Mama suggested that I go out
there anyway so I waited a while thinking that it might slack up
raining some, but it didn't. So, I literally ran out to the car, and
headed to Millington. When I arrived to my surprise people
were coming from all directions, coming in the rain in cab cars.
Coming to defend their pastor, evidently all had heard the news
about what had happened the previous night and they came to
set the record straight. Bro. Hall was presiding when I walked
in, and was he preaching? "Talking about turning off our pastor,
can't nobody turn off our pastor, can't nobody turn off our
pastor. He is here to stay until the Lord moves him." He then
proceeded to give the chair to me, when he presented it to me,
I started thanking everyone who came to support me, and call
for a motion to declare the meeting previously held to be null
and void. Once that was accomplished, Sister Mayrene Hall,
Bro. Hall's daughter rose to make a motion with the preface,
"Talking about turning off our pastor you ain't paying him
anything anyway. I motion that we not only null and void
the previous meeting but I motion that we give our Pastor a

twenty-five dollar a week raise!" It was voted unanimously Bro. Swanson one of the disgruntle ones made the statement "Well you have two churches" to that I responded, "No, no we only have one church and if you are indifferent to that you can get your letter this very moment. Actually, all who want to may receive your letters of dismissal now? Right now, for we do not have but one church, unbelievably, a dog did not wag his tail I then made the statement "you talking about pastorate, I am really going to pastor now from the front door to the pulpit, and any one that stays here is going to obey my every command." I then thanked everybody again and gave the benediction, praise God. However, that was just one indiscretion that happened in the eight-year history of my pastorate at First Baptist Church. For the next five and a half or six years, my pastorate was relatively enjoyable and smooth. It was when I endeavored to seek another pastorate that steered the resentment of those same deacons. Deacon Swanson didn't want to give Mama my little pay when I went out of town one Sunday, but guess what happened; a couple of weeks before I resigned, Deacon Swanson died! His wife knew how he felt about me so she moved the funeral to St. Mark Baptist Church. But one of his daughters came from California and changed the funeral program and put my name on it to preach the eulogy. What a challenging experience that was! But I made fame, a job well done. Bill Boyd the other Deacon, lost his mind and was committed to an institution and died shortly afterwards. The second Sunday of October 1963, I preached my farewell sermon, my dear mother gave me a farewell or going away dinner one evening and invited some first Baptist members, especially those whom she knew loved and appreciated me. That was a glorious occasion, Mama requested that I sing her a song entitled "I am going to leave you in the hands of the Lord." O she really enjoyed that! Even until this day, there are some people at first Baptist that love Pastor Murphy the children, and grand children. They invited me in June *2006 to* carry them into their new edifice. I truly enjoyed seeing and worshipping with those that I knew that there were children when I left First Baptist forty-four years ago, there were those that knew of me who came from near and far just to see me. "And the beat goes on.

"I was in Millington in June of 2007, I stopped at the house where my mother's house was and there was a couple of fellows sitting in the shade under a tree and they recognized me and my goodness, they got on their cell phones, and within minutes people were around my car, there was also a young man that was married to one of my very close friends, Mayrene Hall, daughter whom he said had cancer, and he insisted that I follow him to his house to pray for her, and that I did. It was so thrilling to see the faith that they had manifested toward me. I believe that God healed her, praise God.

So if for Christ I proclaim the glade story if I such for his sheep that gone astray than I know he'll show me his glory when I've gone the last mile of the way. And if here, I have earnestly striven. And have tried all His will to o-bey. Twill en-hance all the rap-ture of heaven. When I've gone the last mile of the way. When I've gone the last mile of the way, I will rest at the close of the day. And I know there are joys that await me. When I've gone the last mile of the way.

Be it so known that there are several accolades, which indicate some of my achievements of which I am very proud of:

1. I was elected Pastor Brown Creek M.B.C. the next year I was elected President of the Brown Creek District Sunday School and B.T. U Congress Association of Christian Education.
2. When elected to Prince of Peace Missionary Baptist Church in Detroit, Michigan a year or so later I was elected

president of the Calvary District Association Sunday School B.T.U. congress of Christian Education of the B.M.E. State Convention of the State of Michigan.
3. I was privileged to serve as presiding official of the Ministers Fellowship of the Full Gospel fellowship of the State of *Michigan.*

Brown's Creek

When God places a burden upon the heart of humanity, it is clear that all of the faculties that are in a person will unite in a concerted effort to aid in the manifestation of the divine order becoming a reality. God has spoken to Pastor Murphy deep within, and now we see how life is becoming a transforming incubator for the man, who has been touched by the Almighty. Preaching for Pastor Murphy has been the quintessence of his ministry, in that he has always focused his textual content toward relevancy. Buried deep within his personhood was the memory of the plantation and the wishes of his grandmother, therefore he used his past experiences with the precision of a sharp shooter placing emphasis upon the power of the God of the universe. Warren H. Stewart shares this with us from his book, *"Interpreting God's Word in Black Preaching"* these words of confirmation, "The Word can only be identified with and experienced when it be understood... preaching, then, must communicate the Word in the common tongue of those to whom the message is directed.....he or she who is involved in effective and accurate hermeneutics in preaching must not confuse his or her primary assignment with that of the theologians and biblical scholars...the preacher must be an effective translator of the Word of God or else his or her mission will be defeated immediately after the text is read."

He recalls these tender moments:

"It is an infallible truth, when it is said the steps of a righteous man is directed by the Lord, as an Insurance man employed by Union Protected Insurance Co, of Memphis Tennessee. I was in the field at work on my debit making my rounds one bright shinning morning, when a preacher friend of mine called me from down the street, waving his hands in the air to get my attention which he did, then he informed me that his home church was vacant and He wanted me to preach for them or become a candidate for the pasturages I readily consented for I was only pasturing second and fourth Sunday which meant that I was available the first and third Sundays, so I suggested that He get me an appointment as soon as possible and because of his believe in my availability and serviceability ect. He went to work and in just a few days, he had accomplished the objective and the appointment secured. It was a first Sunday. Oh, and did we make great impressions, for I acquired the support of the whole First Baptist Church, to accompany me that Sunday. The choir, deacons, ushers, and nurses, it seemed like everybody. (This was for the morning service) Guess what? With First Baptist Church Choir singing, and accompany me, we made such an impression, until Brown Creek members wanted to elect me that Sunday immediately following the Sermon. To do so would have been against the rules, which states "that proper notice to be given for such important business as election of Pastor." Therefore they scheduled a church meeting for the coming Friday evening, and of course they elected me as Pastor unanimous upon receiving the calling I really felt blessed and highly favored of God, I was now a full time Pastor, that is I had some where to preach every Sunday so I felt like I had arrived.

"My pastoral experience at Brown-Creek Church was uniquely different, for her location in the rural of Fayette County Tennessee, which was logically influenced by the Jim Crow plantation concept, as was many of the African American concepts of the lordship slave driver in a concept. The Democratic parliamentarian concept in the rural Church, in most case, can be strongly advocated by the Deacon boards of those Churches. At Brown's Creek Church, such was the case. In fact, every vision or revelation given to the pastor by God for the congregation, would be scrutinized and approved by the board of Deacon's before going to the Church Congregation for their approvable. This required the pastor to be extremely Diplomatic and wise to maneuver successfully, a God given program for the church and the succeed pf the Country preacher depended upon the degree of his Preaching, Singing, Praying, and Pasturing abilities. If he was sensationally and dramatically good, he could get by pretty well. NO BOAST, but that is how, I made it. For many of the things I wanted to do I would just by-pass the Deacons board and go directly to the congregation for approval. I remember so well, the time the transmission went out on my car, which cost Eighty-Five Dollars to repair, monies to which I did not have. Afraid to carry the matter to the Deacons for fear they would not approve, I went directly to the congregation. I knew that they would readily approve. There were those women, like Sis. Ethel Shaw, Sis. Wardell and many others that would as the word goes, "would kill a brick about me." When I put the proposal to the congregation Sis. Shaw immediately stood up and said, "Come on deacons, you heard what he said, he need money to get his car out of the shop!" and before she could finish speaking they had raised more than enough. Overall, I really and truly enjoyed preaching, singing, and praying there, for they loved it as well. I could not wait to get to Brown's Creek on the First and Third Sundays of the month. The facility only seated about three hundred and fifty people, but they would pack that place to hear what thus saith the Lord. O what a day that was the Sunday morning when I offered my resignation. I first told the Deacons in our meeting before the service that this was my last Sunday. I am resigning this morning this is my last Sunday, and when that was said, they began to crying like children. And they questioning as to what they could do to keep me and I had to make it clear that their was nothing that could be done for what was being done was of God. So when we went out to staff the service the people perceived something was wrong, they too started crying. They would not allow me to preach my farewell sermon. Ladies fainted, laid in the isles on pews, on the flowers, everywhere. It was pandemonium. It was a terrible experience, like a funeral. I had to make some tremendous sacrifices while pasturing at Brown's Creek Church, which was seventy-two miles from my home in Memphis. Not that it was a big thing to me at the time a hundred and forty-two miles round trip and many Sundays, I traveled seventy-two miles there, conduct service, preach and drive seventy two miles back to Memphis for a three thirty service for Dr. Abe Campbell and others; then driving seventy-two miles back to Brown's Creek. Conducting evening service and drive back home that night, having spent all of the energy I had. Tired, exhausted, and drained, nothing left physically speaking. I know that serving God would pay after a while. I always believe the scripture that say, he shall loose his or her life for my sake shall find it, and he or she that shall save his or her life shall loose it. I just may be here today, because I have like the Apostle Paul had labored more abounded than them all. I suppose I loved the Browncreek folk so much that whatever sacrifice I had to make was alright. (It did not matter, I was ready for whatever) Brown's Creek Church congregation was much unlike First Baptist Church congregation in that they were compassionate, kind-hearted, and they were always giving my family and I something, cake, pies, canned food you name it, they gave it. So much, so when my grandmother was told that I had resigned, her first reply was, "As nice as those folk are to you; God going to punish you for leaving those peoples." What grandma was thinking about was the chicken, watermelon etc. that they would load up my car with each Sunday."

"After forty four years the bond to love still exists between the Browncreekians and me. As the old saying, "old love never dies". But of course, I don't think that there is one living that were my senior or more, everybody have gone on to be with the Lord, except those that were teenage or younger. But, there are those who remember Pastor Murphy, and there lies the history of W. H. Murphy Sr. and Brown's Creek Missionary Baptist Church."

In this testimony, there is the undoubting faithfulness of a genuine pastor whose love for service to God's people, is in his demonstration of commitment. This is also the results of the divine calling, manifesting itself in such a powerful way, that it will move the person to total submission and obedience. When God speaks to the heart with cooperation of the head, what's orchestrated is provisioned purpose, to bring glory to God in a magnificent way. God's desire is to bring glory and magnification to his name through the totality of human correlation and cooperation. God can do what he pleases, when he pleases but his pleasure is to channel his glory through human copulation. William Henry exemplifies the struggles of humanity with the internal connection of divinity in such a powerful portrait that it behooves anyone to think of God in any other way, than infinite wisdom, deciding to breathe upon finite creatures. William Henry, at this point in his life, has moved from faith to faithfulness. His faith has matured from the plantation, to now planting and watering a congregation that has grown from his faithful stewardship. God always rewards faithfulness are the words that I hear ringing steadily in my head as I recall so many times in my life with him of being unstable and unpredictable. He would constantly remind me that my hard headedness would be my downfall if I did not learn to heed to wise counsel. This has proven to be the case in a many of scenarios that I have had to face as the transformation process continues. Being bull headed and not listening will bring about heartache in every facet of one's life. Now we are not suggesting that William Henry is flawless, but he is definitely faithful, and many times, it is hard to identify the flaws, when one is faithful to the mandate that God has placed upon their lives. The testimony is this, that God will hide your flaws from the critics to bring glory to his name and not our fame. There are those times in our lives that God will allow some things exposed, so that we may return to the state of humility unto him, through respect and reverence. God's desire is to bring us all into the full knowledge of his son and our Lord, Jesus the Christ, and he will do what it takes to mold Christ's character into our character, so that people see more of Him and less of us. God does not change our external before he transforms our internal. The process is always inward first, so that the inner fruit will change the appearance of the outer manifestation of his glory. God is Sovereign and that really means that he is always at work in our lives bring about change for his glory in our story of life.

Chapter 5.

"Ma" Pastor's wife in the Baptist Church

‎﹏

"Momma Murphy! As everyone who knows her calls her, and it is not because of her age. But without a doubt, because of a great show of love, patience, wisdom, stability, and the inapprehensible example of what a pastor's wife and companion should be and all those virtues did not come over night but they are results of many trials, many hardships, many ups and downs, in other words the potter has done what he wanted to do with the clay. And the mold that he put her in, hath made a beautiful vessel." –WHM-

Now these are the words of admiration that William Henry shares about his lovely flower, Mrs. Ella Murphy a.k.a. Mamma Murphy. It stands as this, that a Pastor's wife is a calling as well and to some its experience is felt as though it was a divine intervention. This dynamic duo is without reservation, the kind of love affair one can only dream about. When a man has a calling upon his life, a wife can be a great help and aid, but she can also be a great hindrance and a well capable handicap. However, they defy the odds and walk through life with the steady beat of faithfulness and the assurance of Almighty God resting in their bosoms. William Henry downloads from his heart:

"Mom and I met in August of 1949, on a beautiful Saturday afternoon at a lawn party given by the youth department of her church, just a fine group of young women out to have some clean fun; I am sure I was the only surplanter in the bunch: invited by my cousin to meet another girl. Who was late arriving, which gave me the opportunity to dance with Momma! O boy did I like what I saw, and the way she danced! O boy she could fly around and her little pleated skirt just flared and we really enjoyed each other so much so that I invited her to the movie the very next day which was Sunday evening after church for she was not going to be available until after church. I did not possess the knowledge to anticipate the future I just knew I liked her, and wanted to get married. So I purposed, no engagement ring just popped the question will you marry me, and the answer was yes. So we got married Nov. 27, 1949, on a Sunday afternoon in Sardis, Mississippi. Mom was in High School so we both went back home. Even though we were married, all we had was love, and we did not know at the time that it was Divine Love, we just knew we were in love with each other. Momma had no idea what she was in for as it related to the future, she just liked my mannerism it didn't matter whether we had a place to stay, a bed to sleep in didn't matter just as we long as we had each other and we liked pretty near the same things. I loved to go to the big Band dances, Billy Eckstein, Lonnie Hampton, Duke Ellington, every time a big band came to town, Momma and I would make it our business to attend (what fun). Then the family development began, here comes our first child Carla Diane, then Carolyn Fae, then Corlis Yvonne, the one we lost, and this was a part of the mold the Lord had us in, the lost of a child. O boy, I remember so well what a trauma it was. I was really angry with God until I literally screamed at God (Why did you take my child) the Lord said to me, " How are you going to comfort others if you don't know what its all about." Now when we look within the fabric of this family's consolidated efforts to maintain family solidarity, it has not been pain free but rather its pain's presence has been purposed to produce some poise in their personhood, some progress in their pilgrimage and some pressing to their pace. He continues:

"In addition, he said it in such a way that I knew without a doubt, it was God and immediately I became satisfied. I remember when I called home from work one Tuesday evening after a glorious encounter with God and told Momma, I believe I have been called to preach the gospel her real reply was "I don't want no preacher for a husband", and I quickly replied you may not but you got one, and hung up the phone. When I arrived home that afternoon after work, she had dinner prepared but we never said a word to each other. I sat up until the late show went off for I was scares to death. I guess it was because of what a preacher friend has said to me on my way home on the bus that evening, it so happened that Douglass Malone a minister of our church was on the bus and the only vacant seat was beside him, and I related to him my experience, he said to me: Man I am sure that you have been called but I tell you what when you get home you bow on your knees and tell God to reveal it to you thoroughly because you don't want to make a mistake so I took him at his word and waited until Momma went to bed and when I finally got in bed I could not go to sleep all I could do was preach! Preach, preach, until I decided to get out of bed and tell the Lord I am convinced you have called me to preach now please let me go to sleep for I've got to go to work in the morning I climbed back into bed and calmly went to sleep. My point is Momma had to endure all and everything that was going on between me and the Lord, and O what a going on it was as the Lord taught, brought, and made me, Momma had to make many sacrifices not only having one child after another that she had to care for because if I was not working I was off somewhere preaching a revival etc, which left momma home with the children alone I would leave her for weeks at a time, I am sure she realized just what it necessitate for us to make it, I was determined to make it for a while working from six am to six pm going to night school until 10 pm get home at 10:30 and 11 o'clock nightly which mean Momma was at home at least five days with the children all day by herself. But one of the things about Momma that expressed me among many was her willingness to deny herself for her children. I remember so many times at Easter or Christmas, she would say to me, "Honey don't worry about me just try to get something for the children." My stepmother would give her coats and things to wear. My mother was always jealous of my wife because she loved me so, but she had to confess to me; (one thing about Ella is she takes good care of her children) and that was always with five girls and one boy. In those days Momma would iron those little pleated dresses, comb those five heads and got them ready for church on Sunday after Sunday, and on top of that travel to choir rehearsal, teachers meeting, whatever and sing in the choir and she could really sing. She has to this day a beautiful voice. Much went on in my ministry that was a test to Momma. I remember when I quit my insurance job when I arrived home that early afternoon Momma was surprised to see me. She inquired what I was doing home so early. I said I quit and what did I say that for? She replied in furious anger, "What in the hell do you think we are going to do, starve to death? We aren't doing nothing as it is." My reply was, "I don't give a damn if we all starve to death I am not going back to the job" and stormed out of the door. Well it seemed as if we would starve to death but God took care of us. When it looked like we weren't going to make it, God would step right in just when we needed him most. However what Momma did not know, it was God that told me to quit. I was sitting at my desk pondering over my account which was two cent off and the Lord spoke to me. I know it was Him and he said, "What are you sitting here pondering for, don't you know that I'll take care of you." I was so convinced, that I immediately took my book into the managers' office and gave it to him. He of course pleaded with me to think about it. C.H. Rankins admired my work and wanted me to remain, but God did it.

Nevertheless, Momma because of her love for her family she took it, she persevered, she held on and it took great faith for her to just stay with me. For I have always been a venturous persevering man of great faith, and it took a woman of great faith to follow me, up and down the highways, late at night with all the babies sleep, with one always in her arms. (All I can do to hold back the tears just thinking about all she and I had to endure to make it)

There have been several joyous steps in our lives, for instances my calling to the Prince of Peace Missionary Baptist Church in Detroit, which was a blessing in disguise. At the time of the calling, we were being put out of the apartment, for the lack of payment and the same night we received a telegram saying I had been called to the Church. When I received the telegraph, I literally fell on the floor and praised God, for me it was a blessing. It meant that God was lifting us from poverty. But when I went from Detroit to Memphis, to pick up Mama and my children, that day I shall never forget. It was the twenty-second day of November, nineteenth sixty-three, and the day President Kennedy was assassinated. When I walked in the door, a special news bulletin came on stating that the president had just been assassinated. I took a seat and I sat all afternoon. It wasn't an easy thing for Mom and I to pack up and leave our parents, friends, and loved ones, to move north where we knew no one well, especially for Momma. She had it tough making her mind up to move to Detroit with six children; she had never been to Detroit as I had. I had visited Detroit several times before and had fallen in love with the big country town, I thought it to be a nice city to support and raise a family. Yet Momma did not have that inspiration. All she had was God and confidence in me, who loved her so much, and I thought the sun rose and set in her. Our eight and a half years at Prince of Peace was loaded with changes, challenges, or situations that developed our character, faith, and love for God, and Momma was steadfast through it all. Another severe challenge came when Prince of Peace decided they wanted to dismiss me as pastor. Momma Murphy exercised supreme faith and trust in God; for I don't remember her saying anything negative or voicing any sentiment of distrust. She just took it on the chin, on the Saturday evening that Prince of Peace voted me out as pastor, we were going down the expressway towards home and I was singing, Mama said to me, "Honey why are you singing don't you know they just turned you off and you don't have no church?" I responded, "Honey I am as happy as I ever been in my whole life. Praise God!" It was true; a heavy burden had lifted off of me."

"Between being dismissed from Prince of Peace Church and mobilizing Greater Ebenezer was truly a wilderness experience I realize how Moses felt leading the children of Israel in the wilderness it was a heavy load having people who loved us and wanting to follow us and having no place to go. But, Mama rolled up her sleeves and went to work selling Barbeque Dinners, Chicken Dinners, etc. in order to purchase our first little building at 1184 Grand River, Detroit, Michigan. Mama has become a celebrated scholar and teacher of the book of Revelations and by the aid of the Holy Spirit, she has become an authoritative interpreter of the great book certified by Evangelical Teaching Training Association with full accreditation. Therefore, God has blessed mama exceedingly because of her untiring efforts and undaunted faith with divine health and longevity. Although those "many things" that she was denied in our early marriage, God has given her in her latter days. Now we are praising God for one another. Amen."

The Murphy family has always exhibited a great essence of faith and gravity in the connection of family values. At the center of their family value system is their Christological understanding of how important it is to do all one can to be right in the sight of God and the people of God. Their family core connection is the gravity that "Ella "Ma" Murphy" had from the distillation of what William Henry was faithfully following the leading of the Lord for his family and the Gospel ministry, which was laid upon his bosom. He leads his family with the magnetism of two polarities and she is that opposite polarity that keeps the bond strong. She honed the skills of submission and "learning from her own husband," the importance of possessing the godly character of a saved woman of purpose. Ma Murphy family values were impeccable in her demonstration of excellence at home. (In my, own witness of some twenty-seven years of exposure to "Ma" Murphy, she has always kept a clean house and especially the kitchen and the bathroom. I know this because; I for years worked as a janitor at the church and knew at firsthand how particular Pastor Murphy was about the cleanliness of the Lord's house and his very own home as well.) She has been the pillar of motivation to keep things in order and she always taught the value of hard work and great faith. Her sacrifices were unbelievable at times. She has gone without for many years of the finer things of life and comfort to afford her Pastor, husband, and most of all, her children those creature comforts for the sake of unity and family solidarity. It will be noted, that she wore the same coat for many years, with only having to have the lining restored a few times in over twenty years of ministry and family life.

Her walk of faith has help nurture the fruit of a black Baptist heritage, which has been matured in her loving arms and her undoubting sternness with whom all that she has touched. "Ma Murphy" has given to the black Baptist church a model of faith in the office of the Pastor's wife. When we suggest office, it is because she has given to the black Baptist church her all, as it related to her patience, faith, love, long- suffering and her life. We say office for she has functioned in so many capacities within the texture and fabric of the church, that at times we wondered how well she could speak on behalf of the Pastor, for at times in his absence, she has relayed his thoughts, ideas, and visions very clearly. When a wife takes these active roles in the process of vision demonstrating, she has at heart a love for God and a love for her husband that is unmatched. There is nothing publicly known outside of her own person, of her internal ministry with the Lord. She helps us all, to harness and guard that special place with and for the Lord that even her husband for over fifty plus years dares not tread upon. She lets us all know that the Lord needs to have a place in all of us that is his alone. This holy ground is where one can go and commune with the Lord regardless of the external turmoil that we could be experiencing. No matter the possible appearance of external turmoil her Pastor and Husband may have been faced with, at the churches he pastured, "Ma Murphy" has stood as a pillar of faith. There is no place in this writing to discuss the internal struggles, hardships, joys, and progresses of their marriage, yet we all know that there is only one perfect marriage that is ever going to take place and that is with Christ and his unspotted, wrinkle free, unblemished Church. Therefore, the confidentiality and the sacredness of their holy matrimony must be kept untainted and unblemished, and must be kept for and to them and the Lord. Our focus is to protract from their faithfulness and their solidarity as a single family unit and not to display, discuss or criticize any flaws that may or may not have been known. We protect their family values by doing this and demonstrate our love for them and the Lord. "What God has joined together, let no man pull apart, divide or cause any disturbance." Listen to William Henry share with us the faithfulness of "Ma Murphy."

"Ella was very reluctant to leave Memphis. I think mainly because, she did not know anyone in Detroit and we were leaving all of her relatives and friends behind. The move surely requested great faith to pack up and move north with six children, but again we had no place to go and we were going to be outdoors."

It takes a faith in God to leap at this kind of venture without any guarantees or a back up plan. Life pulls at us with these kinds of difficult choices when it comes down to following the leading of the Lord and the sake of keeping the unity of the family. The question can be asked of all of us, who try to do what we think the Lord is leading us to do for him. Like our father of faith, Abraham, who was asked to leave the familiar to undertake the unfamiliar, with only the voice of the Lord as his guarantee and back up plan, this family moves to the north, to a city of possibility and uncertainty. Detroit was known as the "Motor City" because of the "Big Three" Automakers were some of the largest employers of African Americans. How do we explain this kind of family solidarity in the midst of the possibility of failure and ultimate demise? How do we access this walk of faith during the sixties and the turbulence with our nation and the people of color? Many people from the southern region migrated to northern city like Detroit. Many of these southerners knew first hand what it was like to work hard and the enticing draw for a better life presented the golden opportunity to leave the south and its painful past and start anew in the "Big" city.

Chapter 6.

Obeying the Divine Calling while Responding to Visions and Revelations

⟶

"Through the fire and through the need to achieve experience, knowledge, and faith. Truly, our Heavenly Father will carry us through the wilderness of encounters before reaching the kingdom. Without the wilderness encounters we are not fit for Canaan."

"The wilderness experience is God's way of qualifying us for Kingdom building the reason I am relaying this thought is because, I have been through so much so many valley's so many astronomical challenges in my life to the extent at times I thought I was gone or it was over. When I look back over my life through self examination to find aspects of my character that determined where I am today, my conclusion is that my faith is responsible, my faith in God has caused me to do some strange things, such as quitting my job and trusting God to make a way for me to provide for my family for instance sitting at my desk and tabulating my account as an insurance man or underwriter, my account was 1 cent off so I sat back in my chair pondering, my Lord, I sent off I wonder where in the world that one cent could be as I wondered, the Lord said to me with clarity and distinction, why are you sitting here don't you know that I will take care of you the voice was so convincing that the sound there of caused chills to run all over me. I immediately closed the book cleaned off my desk went into the managers office and put the book on his desk and said, "I am quitting". My goodness the look on his face was astonishing with amazement, he replied, "What's wrong did someone do something to you?" I said, "No I am just quitting". So he responded, "Well take a couple of weeks think about it, them let me know." I knew I would not be back and I could not tell him what had happened he would not believe me if I told him so I just said, "I quit." I left the insurance office went home all I could here was why are you sitting here don't you know I will take care of you? When I arrived at home and opened the door went in, my wife Ella was surprised to see me at that time of the day so she asked what are you doing home this time of the day? I responded I quit my job, and what did I say that for she was disgusted and with displeasure she replied, " You what, what in the hell you think we are going to do, we are about to starve to death as it is now", and of course I responded with much anger, "I don't give a damn if we all starve to death, I am not going back to that job", and then I proceeded to walk back out the door." Now to some this would appear to be a struggle against each other, but this is the consolidation of their faith, working through a tough decision to follow the leading of God. On one hand, there is the concern of a wife and mother, whose position totally correct, but on the other hand, there is the mandate from heaven on the man, the husband, and the provider. When God calls upon the soul and the spirit, who can explain, who can divest that holy unction? When God calls, how shall we respond? When God calls, how shall we answer? When God calls, how do we explain to those the closes to us, that what we have to do, may be painful to the equilibrium of our family. When God calls, he expects a rapid response to the drum beat of his voice, how do we explain that to everyone else, who did not hear what he said to you? William Henry has to dig deeper into his inner self to tap into an unknown resource that is nestled at the core of his faith. He has to walk the walk, while he is talking the talk. William Henry goes deeper. Tune in:

"Faith to the faithlessness is always interpreted as foolishness. This act of faith, subjected us to many difficulties just to acquire the necessities of life we really hit rock bottom. Even though I was pasturing two churches, First Baptist and Brown's Creek and between the two I was receiving less than two hundred dollars per month which was far less than what was needed to support a family of eight people, even in the early sixties." How do you explain to your family that the suffering that they and you are enduring is a divine mandate. It is hard enough to see yourself having to go through this, but to carry your family through this can be a heartbreaker and a spirit crusher

"It is true that the number of our family size served as a motivator to encourage us; and did so to me in all my endeavors. Mama and I were blessed with one child after another or one immediately after the other. I suppose it was because we really loved and cared for and esteemed each other and made each other happy. This drove me to seek a better life for us, so whenever the opportunity presented a chance to preach at a larger Church I seized the privilege."

Chapter 7.

Prince of Peace

~~~

In the life and times of William Henry, there has been some very unique and divinely charged events that have infused his faith in the power of God. Dependency on God and being able to walk by faith and not by sight can give one a since of arrogance and humble obedience in the Lord. It is then that one can garner hope in hopeless situations. A faith walk with God will fortify one's faith in the power of the risen Lord, which will empower the heart to tackle any obstacle and stand strong in the Lord. William Henry moves with the precision of a surgeon and gentleness of a ballet dancer through the wilderness experience he has to endure at the fate of a church whose understanding is not totally clear as to the agenda of the Almighty. This exposure to the city of Detroit helps to solidify his footing that God had ordained him to be a gifted preacher, full of the assurance and the anointing power of the Holy Spirit to do ministry for the twenty-first century.

He recalls:

"I became the quest of Pastor John L. Webb in Detroit, MI when the opportunity came to preach at Prince of Peace, as has been said earlier. God ordered Prince of Peace to call me just in time, things were critical for me and Ella that is financially, we could not even pay rent to keep a roof over our heads."

"John L. Webb sent for me to preach for him the first Sunday of February 1963. I did not even have bus fare to Detroit so John L. as his closet friends called him, sent thirty-five dollars for me to come to Detroit byway of the city of New Orleans. My ticket cost twenty-seven dollars one way after which I had seven dollars left and I was afraid to spend a nickel. I remember I had no lunch and between Memphis and Chicago, I became so hungry it seemed I would starve to death. I held out as long as I could, finally I decided to go to dinner and see what I could purchase for a reasonable price according to what I had to spend. I made my way to the diner and looked down the isle. All I could see was white folks and I was not use to sitting and dining with white folks. There was only one seat vacant and that was face to face with a well-dressed rich looking white man. I braced myself leaned over to him and somehow I asked the question, "sir do you mind if I sit here" surprisingly he welcomed me with a smile," surely he replied come on join me." Therefore, I took a seat looking at the menu to see what I could order at a reasonable price to satisfy my hunger. That hamburger cost three dollars and fifty cents so I ordered."

"The man was reading a newspaper about the missile crisis between John F. Kennedy and Soviet Leader Nikita Khrushchev. He decided to discuss it with me (by the way he asked what you think about the missile crisis). Well, I was in College at the time and one of my subjects just so happened to be, political Science and as a test, I was required to do a paper on the missile crisis, so I was able to hold a decent conversation with the man. Another reason I think the man was so open to me is, while sitting down, then I proceeded to introduce myself. I extended my hand and said I am W. H. Murphy of Memphis, Tennessee and of course, he gave me his hand and told me his name J.A. Martin. By then we finished that course of conversation, when I had finished my sandwich, the man looked at me and said are you going to have dessert? I replied no, and he quickly replied "Go ahead, order some dessert, as thin as you are you could us it anyway." he continued, "I am going to pay for it, anyway." He suggested that I order a banana split and so I did, boy was it good. When I finished, I thanked him and started to exit when he said here take my card and if ever you need me call me. Unknowingly to me the man was President of the First National Bank of New York City. Well what you know, I misplaced the card I was unable to ever contact the man."

"I shall never forget that Saturday morning when the readout sheriff was next door setting the family three doors down from me out on the streets, I stood in my doorway praying Lord please don't let them set me and my children out on the streets for I had prioritized the best I could and food came first then rent. Therefore, Ella, and I decided to put our furniture in storage and move with her aunt Annie Mae until we could do better, so when the sheriff finished setting my neighbors out, he and his crew came to my door. The sheriff asked who I was, I replied I am Reverend Murphy, he quickly responded, "I am supposed to set you out," and I said in as humble tone of voice as I could, "Mister. Please don't set me out for I plan to pay my rent Monday." He looked at me and said, " I am not suppose to do that and I can get in trouble doing so, but do you sincerely promise if I let you stay that you will pay the rent Monday," with a voice of exuberate I replied, "Yes sir I promise." "Okay," he replied, "don't get me in trouble." and he turned and walked away telling his crew come on we are finished for the day, and of course I proceeded to praise the Lord for I well knew that it was God's doing for that white man could care less about my situation. Mama (Ella) and I continued to pack our belongings, for we knew we would not have the rent money by Monday, therefore we proceeded with our plans to move. "

"I am sure you have heard the old saying or cliché, "he may not come when you want him but he is always on time", well the saying is none the less true, he may not come when you won't him but he's always on time. That same Saturday night about 7:30 p.m. my doorbells rang and guess what a telegram from Prince of Peace Baptist church the telegram read, "The Board of Deacons, Pulpit Committee, and Members have unanimously elected you as pastor as long as you, and the Church can agree", and that was the usual procedure in those days. As long as Pastor and Church could agree. My what a great rescue, what a great blessing that was one of the greatest achievements in my whole life; I was so thankful to God so greatly elated thrilled inspired emotionally stirred that I fell prostrate on the floor praising God for the calling it meant the way out of poverty and suffering for me and my six children. The usual procedure for accepting the calling to a vacant church was to go before the congregation and announce or preach an acceptance sermon that I did not have much time to do. I had to move quickly for implementing the plains which included accepting the church member now this is the first Saturday in October 1963, that very first Sunday I went to Brownsville and resigned the Church and I went to Millington the second Sunday in October and resigned First Baptist Church, and the third Sunday of October I went to Detroit to except Prince of Peace and have a Board meeting. In that meeting we discussed the affaires of Church in general including the budget I remember so well Brother Leroy Chapman statement concerning my financial support (quote), "We can not give you a salary all we can do is take care of you and your family we guarantee that you and your family will not want for anything. In this condition, I was glad to be so secure. Praise God, the Board of Deacons and I begin planning my installation to raise monies to move my family and me to Detroit and get us a place to stay. We planned for the installation to conclude the second Sunday in November 1963 and of course we planned to journey to Tennessee to get my family the fourth week in October we would rent a large truck and one large car and drive a car to bring the children so on the twenty-fifth of November we started out to Tennessee we arrived at mama Ella's aunt's house at 1311 south Willet at approximately 3:30 p.m. Time I walked into the house there came a special bulletin the President of the United States of America had just been assassinated. "Lord have mercy on us, especially us black folks." For we had hopes that he would be the one that would up grade our civil rights privileges and now our hopes are shattered what an awful evening that was, November 25, 1963. I took a seat and I did not move for at least three hours, what a heart breaking encounter that sad news projected truly a day to remember. Well thee next day we went to the storage company picked up the furniture and then Ella and the kids and headed back to Detroit, oh yes the last stop was my mother's home at Millington Tennessee twelve miles north of Memphis, really that is where I was born. My mother did not want me to go north, she felt like my health could not stand the climate, so she wept and pleaded with the deacons to please take care of her son, practically Brother Griffin and he promised her that he would take care of her son." Ella was very reluctant to leave Memphis I think mainly because she didn't know any one in Detroit and was leaving all of her relatives and friends behind. The move surely requested great faith to pack up and move north with six children but again we had no place to go we were out doors."

The Board of Deacons, at Prince of Peace moved us into one of the members apartments complex with two bedrooms, kitchen and living room, with the understanding that they would as soon as possible purchase us a home, but the fact of the matter was they never intended to do so; my thinking is that they did not plain to do anymore than what they had orig-inally promised and that was me and my family would have food to eat and a roof over our heads and no more. Before they moved us into that apartment at 3850 31st Street owned by the Anders family who were members of the church, they promised to purchase a house but after moving us into the apartment the honeymoon, was over. Honestly speaking we were never treated so royal and kind before they were really nice to me and my family I remembered the first Christmas here in Detroit as pastor my children had the best Christmas ever before, because the members of the Church teamed up and purchased gifts for each of my six children. Oh, what a time those kids had, with all their new stuff. One of the Deacons came by the apartment and mama was washing cloths in the bathtub by hand because we had no washing machine he went immediately and purchased one and had it delivered to the apartment. Another observed that we had but one television, went and purchased one and had it delivered to the apartment. Praise God! This was one act of kindness after another but again I say the honeymoon didn't last long for as soon as I started exercising my power and authority by making new rules and procedures for instance all treasures was asked to report their monies to the main treasure of the Church in order to secure the Church's monies boy o' boy what did I do that for man o' man that certainly raised some feathers, following my ruling I was going down to the base-ment cafeteria one Sunday morning while the Deacons were having coffee and they didn't know that I was standing on the stairwell so one of them said to the other fellows, "Man we got to do something about this nigger pastor. He done took away our spending money." They all chuckled and laughed, and of course, when I walked down among them there was a funny look on their faces. That was the beginning of a tremendous reversal in the church a struggle for power as to who was going to run the church the deacons or me.

The deacons started doing those things that they knew was against or to my disliking for instance I was supported financially by love offering and my love offering would average from ninety five too sixty five dollars per week in the sixties that wasn't to bad, but then that amount started dwindling to the extent I called a meeting and asked for a salary increase of seventy five dollars per week and of course they were surprised and reluctant for they didn't think that I had the nerves, but I did so to extend my income. I threatened them with and ultimatum by saying if you don't give it to me this will be my last Sunday; they paused for a moment and one of them said you heard what the man said give it to him so they voted unanimously to give me the fixed salary. Well, even at seventy-five dollars per week it was hard for me to make it with six children in school just to keep them looking decent etc. It was a thing of living from hand to mouth as the old cliché goes; I would borrow money from who ever I thought had some and would not be hesitant about loaning it to me. I would determine, who I was going to borrow from each Monday morning just to buy groceries the reason I had to borrow on Monday is because I would have paid out my little monies to those whom I had borrowed from the previous Monday, so on Sunday night I came home and started thinking about who I was going to borrow from this week, while thinking on the matter the Holy spirit said pray about it; so I got down on my knees and begin to pray Lord I am tired of borrowing money and living like this please show me a way, to better support my family. Would you believe that very next morning Pastor Sam Turner called me and after salutation asked me the question, "Man he said don't you have a degree in underwriting?" I replied by saying I have a certificate from Tennessee State in underwriting he then informed me that the General Electric Co. had been sited for violation of equal opportunity labor law and needed to hire an African American, he further advised me to go and ask for a Mr. Bush at a Community Center on fourteenth street I took his advice and Mr. Bash sent me immediately to general electric Co. located on East Nevada St. and they hired me Johnnie on the spot and of course that was the beginning of mama and I rising from poverty to God supplying our every need according to his riches in glory Phil 4:19."

"Mama went to work as a Doctor's assistant for Dr. John W. Moore on Eight Mile Road, so we put our monies together and saved our monies and then started looking for us a house, of course this is five years later it is now 1968. We closed the deal on our first house January 1, 1968. We were not able to move in until July of that year. However, that new house located within a particularly all white neighborhood, further fanned the fuel of the envious, jealously and selfishness on the part of the Prince of Peace Deacons. This is what took place; we gave a house warming party and invited the whole church out to celebrate the goodness of God. Our thinking was they would surely be proud that their Pastor and his family would have a nice home to live in, was we in for a great surprise. The evening of the house warming, one of the Deacons remarked to another Deacon, "Man I've been up here for years and worked everyday and I don't live in a house like this." From that house warming, the battle was intensified. They started meeting from house to house and scheming up ways to get rid of their Pastor. The war came to a climax, Saturday December 12, 1971. Nevertheless, the year before in 1970, we had a church meeting and I left that meeting all discouraged and distorted because everything that I had planned to offer to the Church for the advancement of the ministry, the Deacons screened and voted against it. Therefore, when I made it to the church, I had nothing to offer, such as I was recommending that we purchase a bus to transport the congregation when we went on outings and especially the youth, which had not transportation. The deacons voted it down for said they, "We had a bus and it sat out there in back of the church and the kids broke all of the windows out of it, so we don't need no bus." I also wanted a broadcast and had went to various properties and solicited their weekly financial support and collected the first months payments and the deacons rejected that proposal their reasons were; that they once had a broadcast and ending up owing a huge balance so they voted it down. When the closure of the deacons meeting, I went out to meet with the church, I had nothing left to offer them. I was so angry when I left that church meeting while I was going down the Lodge Freeway heading homeward, I said to God in an angry tone, "Lord you can either straighten out these folks or you move me! And I mean it." The Lord replied with no uncertain terms, "Ok I will fix it for you." My, did He fix it." All hell broke out with those people, that I knew loved me, now had turned against me. Mother Harris, for instance, that woman would give me the cloths off her back, and I didn't have to ask for it she would ask; have you any money if I said no she would quickly reach in her purse and hand me what she thought I needed and would ask is that enough, same way about food; questions are you hungry can I fix you something to eat and if I said yes she would immediately start cooking or preparing me something to whether it was breakfast, lunch or dinner that's just how she was concerning me I was her son. But I saw that lady change her attitude towards me over night Saturday evening December 12, 1971 when at our annual church meeting they dismissed me from the pasturage we were in the Deacons meeting and they allowed her to sit in which was against the rules but that's just how influential she was no one was going to ask her to move or leave, each of the Deacons was voicing there opinions about the relationship that is between Pastor and them and their main objective was they didn't wont as they said all of the dancing in the church so one Deacon replied; "This is not a sanctified church so you ought take all of these folks and start your own Church." I quickly responded by saying I have been praying that God would breath on us in such away as evidence of his presence so he answered my prayer. At that time mother Harris raised her hand and I gave her the permission to speak and I remembered so plainly she made the statement I agree with these Deacons I interrupted, Mother, is that the way you feel? Because I was shocked, I could not believe Mother was saying those things and she replied that is just the way I feel we trusted the Deacons to go down in Tennessee and get you and bring you up here and we trust them now. With her finger pointed at me and of course, that was the wrong thing for her or any one to do. I preached her funeral the next month.

The next month than one of the Deacons spoke out and suggested that I resign, to that I quickly said, "I can not do that, for I promise God I would never renege on a Divine assignment: but you can turn me off." One of them said, "Come on you all, lets go out here and turn him off." I responded, "Go on out, start the meeting and I'll be on out." So they did, when I perceived that devotion was over, I went out took my place as Pastor. I then preceded to the podium addressed the congregation and made this statement. "Well I guess there is no use in me offering my God given program for the next fiscal year?" someone yelled out, "No." you wont need one" I said then are you ready to declare the pulpit vacant the answer came readily yes then said I will entertain a motion to that effect what happened, they had to meet at the home of Mother Harris that early afternoon to map out strategies for the meeting so they new just who would make the motion and everything so Boatwright loudly stated I motion that the pulpit be declared vacant Cara Thomas loudly said I second that motion I then established a committee to do the counting, the tally was ninety two to thirty seven which meant the pulpit was declared vacant I made the statement the pulpit is declared vacant so you do not have a pastor, are you prepared to pay me?" The agreement was in the case the pastor and the Church could not agree the Church would have to pay me ninety days in advance. Someone yelled, "Yes give him his money and let him get out of here" but there were those Prince of Peaceians whom God had left to love me: were in an uproar, I wouldn't let anyone speak, only one exception and that was mother Wilson, I recognized her, she stood up with tears streaming down her cheeks and said, "You all don't know what you have just done, you have just turned off Jesus; and then took her seat."

"The majority of the people that were present, I had never seen before in the nine years, I had been Pastor, they seemed to have come from nowhere. But one thing for sure I was so relieved when the count was finished and I was no more pastor of Prince of Peace Baptist church. I was sick and tired of those people and I felt like God was answering my prayer, for I had told God in the midst of frustration please straighten these people out or move me and I mean it, to that God replied ok I'll fix it for you, and he did I saw all hell break out so I felt like God was answering my prayers. I went home down the expressway, singing thank-you Lord I just want to thank-you Lord, my wife asked me honey are you crazy; here you are singing don't you know those people just turned you off, and you don't have no church I quickly replied Honey I feel better than I have ever felt in my life, and that was the truth for it seemed as if a load lifted of me, praise God." "Moreover, the beat goes on."

Chapter 8.

Dr. Murphy breaks from Tradition (Without Breaking the Mode) The Birth of Greater Ebenezer Missionary Baptist Church

During the time after the events that took place at Prince of Peace in Detroit, God transitioned Pastor Murphy's ministry dynamics to see that his anointing was unique and different. He moves "out of the Box," from the traditional traps that would snare his progress into new territories. With this understanding, there was the need, we see now, for God to expose Pastor Murphy to the spiritual high places in the eyes of many witnesses his divine mandate. He would as time would present itself, be different and unique in his approach to doing ministry. The painful past of Prince of Peace Church, generated a theological thrust with a charismatic flow into the mindset of Pastor Murphy. He discerning eyesight into the lives of the God's creation, stirs a fever in him for lost souls. His evangelistic outlook goes deep within his spirit. Listen as he opens his heart:

"I went home that Saturday night and slept like a log, all the way through Sunday. We had planned a concert for that Sunday night and all my children were singing. I did not go, that was the first time I had missed Church on Sunday except when I was ill. That Sunday evening Preachers heard the news and gathered at my house. Especially close friends, Dr. John Webb, Dr. Herbert Hinkle, and Dr. M.B. Brown. Several other Pastors' sympathized with me. They were concerned as to how I would make it, now that I had no church to pastor. They did not know that mama and I had put away for a rainy day. I accepted a good position with General Electric Co. For a while, we were well fortified. I had decided I was going to take my time and figure out what town I wanted to live and pastor in. I felt like according to my experience, education, status, and gifts of the Holy Spirit I could make a choice and be in charge. We were sitting in my family room chit chatting and the phone keep ringing. Mama would answer it finally; John L. Webb with seriousness of tone pointed his finger at me and said, "Man if you don't organize these people the Lord is going to punish you." When he said that the Holy Spirit went through me like a bolt of lightening and the phone rang. Mama said "honey its Mrs. Ross; she wants to know what are you going to do." I replied, "Tell her to meet here tomorrow evening." From that point on, mama would tell everyone who would enquire to meet tomorrow evening to discuss mobilization."

"Monday December 14th 1971 eight people met in our family room to discuss mobilizing a body of Christ, an Ecclesia. I cannot remember all eight who were present. I know Mrs. Ross, George Matthews, and my family and I was all there. We formulated plans for the new body of Christ Jesus our Lord and Savior. There was a young man present, named James H. Mosley that I perceived had great potential as a preacher. Samuel Berry Jr. who was our minister of music at Prince of Peace was also present. After formulating plans for the Ecclesia, we announced a meeting for December 15 to mobilize. There were 54 people present, 23 adults and the others were children. We did not know just who to expect or who was interested in such a movement or following me as a Pastor. We hugged and greeted each other with love and excitement. There were those Pastors present whom I did not expect. Such as, Pastor Griggs of Second Ebenezer, Pastor Samuel Berry, Pastor John L. Webb of New Mount Vernon and several others. We met at Joy Road.

"A real estate man called me Sunday night upon hearing what had happened. He seized the opportunity to sell me the building on Joy Road, which was the old Metropolitan Church of God in Christ. He gave us the privilege to meet there and I perceived it to be a blessing from God. I felt like God was making a way for the new Church organism. The building was too much for our small group so we met on December 15 and mobilized. The night of putting together an operative Christian organization within the organism was a tremendous under taking. First, there needed to be qualified persons for each ministry present. Such as Deacons, trustees, ushers, mothers, nurses, Superintendent of Sunday School, Baptist Training Union. Of course, there was not one qualified person present. Therefore, we appointed the best person available for each position. For instance, Mrs. Wilma English was appointed the first Superintendent of Sunday School. Sister Louise Thomas was the Chairman of Trustees. Robert Hughes was the first trial Deacon. Suzie Briggs was the first nurse. Sister Lucille Wilbourne was the first mother appointed. Each person who would also become a part of the Board of Directors, which would operate the whole Church. The question arose as to what we would name the new Church. Several names were suggested, but I had already decided that I wanted to name her Ebenezer Missionary Baptist Church. When I suggested that name Rev. Briggs made the statement that we could not name her that because there was an Ebenezer in the city already. He stated that there was not only an Ebenezer but there was an

Ebenezer African Apostolic Church. His church was Second Ebenezer, but he said you could name her Greater Ebenezer Missionary Baptist Church. Everybody unanimously approved. I was so happy because I came out of Ebenezer Baptist Church in Memphis Tennessee. That's where I was called to preach, licensed, and ordained by the late Dr. E. L. Slay. The name meant in 1st Samuel 7:12, God is our Stone help. I was very fond of that name, praise God."

"The Apostolic Congregation moved us out without notice, which placed upon me the responsibility to find us a place to Worship. What a trauma that was, trying to find a building to our satisfaction. It would take time, days or even weeks to find a suitable place. We needed some place to congregate immediately. We had several offers; of course, one was Dr. Webb. He extended an invitation for us to worship with him at New Mount Vernon Baptist Church. We did baptize with him and his congregation the first Sunday evening of the New Year, but I did not will not to worship with Dr. Webb on a consistent bases. Therefore, we decided to worship with one of my sons in the ministry, Pastor Jessie Calimesa at Greater Beulah on Eight Mile and Wyoming. It was a real nice church building. We started worshiping with them the second Sunday in January that was a phenomenal challenge for all of us that demanded prayer, devotion and commitment, operating in such made all go well, and the Calimesa's were nice people they truly made us feel at home in fact they went out of their way to do so; Rev. Calimesa gave me the privilege to preach every other Sunday. I would preach the first and third Sunday and he would preach second and fourth Sunday; all went well the Lord was with us to sanction the fellowship we would also receive our offering at the same time, representatives from each Church. Sunday School, morning worship whatever, when we would extend the invitation or call to discipleship we would announce both names Greater Beulah and Greater Ebenezer but surprisingly everybody wanted to unite with Greater Ebenezer and we were the guest and I think because of that Rev. Calimesa was influenced to make his decision to resign his Church and turn the building and his people over to me. It was the second Sunday in February 1972 during Sunday school, he approached me and asked if I would meet with him in his office. I agreed when he preceded to his office he beaked for Mrs. Calimesa; when we arrived in his office, he begin to speak his intentions he said. "Rev I have prayed over this matter and the Lord want me to turn this Church over to you." Than he looked at Mrs. Calimesa for approval "Isn't that right honey", she replied, "yes." We prayed about it and that's what the Lord wants us to do." He then stated that he would be my assistant, If I wanted him too or he would just leave. While he was talking, I was thinking and as soon as he finished I immediately replied, " I can not do that," with shock and dismays, Rev. I am serious, I really mean it that's what the Lord wants me to do, I still said I can not do that, really I didn't know why, I just knew I couldn't do that, here the man is offering me his building and his people and with my people. The house is full in every service, but the answer was, "no I can not do that", that was the end of that conversation. At this juncture, I didn't know what we would do or which way we would go, we had the responsibility to not only look for a place we could call our own but also we had to save money to purchase a place for worship, but I new I could not accept Rev. Calimesa offer. Every time I look back on the situation, I've come to the conclusion that God was testing me so that I could come to the knowledge of right direction to travel."

Our First Place of Worship:

Mrs. Suzie Briggs called me one weekday to tell me of a building that was for sale and she was all inspired and optimistic about the location it was located on Grandriver at Kentucky 12000 Grandriver owned by Bishop Brooks of the New St. Paul Church of God In Christ. Bishop Brooks and his congregation was moving to Oakman and Joy Road, so I called the Bishop for an appointment to see the building. He responded by giving us an appointment that Saturday at 1:00 p.m. There was several other places that we wonted to see so we made the Grandriver site last, when we walked in 12000 Grandriver that afternoon Bishop Brooks was sitting in his little pulpit area awaiting our arrival. We therefore surveyed the building. After doing so, we all agreed that this would be an ideal place for us to start, just the right location plus the building had installed pews and an elevated choir stand and pulpit dieses. We were inspired. I then proceeded to talk business with the Bishop. I suggested that we rent with option to buy for one year. We would give him two thousand dollars down, monthly payment of three hundred dollars per month for one year, at the end of the year we would give him the balance of five thousand more a total of nineteen thousand dollars then we would enter into a land-contract for ten years to pay the balance total fifty five thousands dollars, the Bishop gave me his word that we would discuss the transaction with his board and would let me know his decision as soon as possible, sure enough he did. His board approved. We closed the deal and made ready to move in the fourth Sunday in February 1972, as Bishop Brooks moved out that same Sunday we were moving in. O, what a great date that was here we were moving into our own building we were free to do God's will by the aid of the Holy Spirit praise God.

Indeed, we moved into our own place of worship and began the work of canvassing and evangelizing the community, I knocked on so many doors they thought I was a Jehovah witness that I am but only through Jesus Christ our Lord. One Saturday morning I was out there witnessing on Walbash Street. I walked up on a woman's porch and knocked on the door. The lady came to the door screaming get off of my porch, I threw up my hands and replied but lady I am a Baptist preacher I am pastor Murphy, Pastor of Greater Ebenezer Missionary Baptist Church right here on Grandriver, the lady then apologized for she thought I was a Jehovah Witness that same day I knocked on the Gillings door and Senya their baby daughter came to the door. I asked her were her parents at home. She exclaimed, "They are not here." I then placed a flyer through the door telling her to give it to her parents and I would be looking for them at Church the coming Sunday. Sure enough that Sunday, Mrs. Gillings came to Church and joined and from then, many of her family members, also joined. God sent people from the north, south, east, and west. Our greatest number per Sunday to receive was seventy-two and that was first Sunday. That evening, we baptized sixty- seven of the seventy-two that united and of course, each and every Sunday we would receive twenty-five or thirty-five or more. Evangelism was the order of the day. We purchased a sixty-passenger bus of which we had no driver but me. I would for many Sundays go over the city of Detroit all the way to the east side in fact as far as Conner Avenue to pick up people for Sunday School, bring them to Church, teach then preach, get back upon the bus carry them back to the east side go home to Lauder Street eat my dinner take a nap get back upon that bus pick the people up again for Baptist training union and Church on first Sunday I would do all that plus baptize and issue Holy Communion get on that bus carry the people home after preaching to them two and three times that day. Sometimes I would not get home on Sunday nights until twelve and one o'clock that is if the bus did not break down. Many Sunday nights, that was the case the bus would break down any where it didn't have no preferences just anywhere. Several times, I had to call for members with cars to come get the people and carry them home. What a drama but I endured the cross despise the shame for I was determined to be successful. I would not have it said that I had not done my job; so I labored more abundantly than them all; O how mystical the Lord dealt with me doing the time of the infancy of Greater Ebenezer. I had no idea to the dimension; that is the spiritual dimension, that God wanted to carry me in ministry in fact God freed me from the traditional Baptist Church and his domination authority in the church such as the Board of Deacons, Board of Trustees who in most Church's controlled everything including the Pastor, which is contrary to biblical teaching, Acts 20:28.

Again, the Lord freed me from such so that he could use me to serve as a pioneer for the deliverance of his people from Satan's power with the laying on of hands, anointing with oil and just plainly calling and demanding Satan to leave from the indwelling of God's people. It all started one Wednesday evening. I went to my office to read a book that I was interested in. Then I went to my office about eleven o'clock a few minutes after I arrived Pastor Charles Milton called. I was happy to hear from him, he wanted to know what I was doing. I told him I was reading a book he then wanted to know how long I would be there. I told him I would be there for a while, soon afterwards, he arrived with a cassette tape by Kenneth Copeland talking about the power of faith. Milton and I really enjoyed discussing the subject matters to the extent that time just slipped away. When I knew it was almost four o'clock so I said to Charles, " It's almost four o'clock and I am going home to get my dinner. Mama always had dinner ready about four o'clock. I invited him to go home with me but he declined as we proceeded to leave the office, I said to Milton, "What are you doing tonight?" He replied, "Nothing in particular!" I said,

"Why don't you come and teach us that lesson tonight for we have a young lady that I ask to come to prayer meeting tonight that we may pray for her. She is going to the hospital tomorrow for open-heart surgery and the doctors said that she only have a fifty-fifty chance. Before I could finish that statement the phone ring and it was her on the phone. She wanted to know was we still going to have prayer meeting. I gave her an empathic, "Yes," for I knew we was going to experience a glorious worship experience. The lady's request gave me a change of mind, I then told Milton, " I believe I'll stay here and call some of our members in order to make sure we had a competent ordinance." So I went back into my little office and started dialing telephone numbers. First, I called mama to inform her that I wasn't coming home for dinner and to bring me something. She gave an encouraging, "Okay." We had made a directory of all church members, which was a bit over two hundred. Therefore, I start calling the A's and when I realized it was seven o'clock and the people that I had called from the A's were coming in the door and soon the place was full. We started our usual service with praise and prayer and the meditation of the word. I then introduced Milton and he started talking about faith, its definition, power,and results. Oh, what a mighty word it was when Milton finished speaking he then proceeded to lay hands on the people for healing and deliverance and the irre- sistible power of God was undeniable the Holy Spirit was slaying nearly everybody that would summit. O what a time when Milton finished I took over in amazement and aston- ishment for I had never experienced anything like that in my whole ministry. So after I somewhat got my composure, I proceeded to receive the offering. I remember so well the offering was sixty-seven dollars, I suggested that we make it seventy-five dollars. Deacon Carl Barner raised his hand for those that would give the people responded in a matter of minutes the amount suggested was accomplished."

"O-Boy, O-Boy all at once two young ladies stood upon the pews stared at one another and began to make funny noises, their hair stood up on their heads, their complexion changed, their eyes turned blood red, and they screamed like panthers, they started clawing each other, therefore, we had to get between them to keep them from fighting each other. I have never seen such excitement in all my life everybody is wondering what in the world is going on, What is God doing? If it is God at all. Milton recognized what was happening he came out of the office looked and immediately acted and started speaking with authority saying, Hey Satan, what are you doing in here? When he said that the demons got uncontrollably worse Milton didn't give up any grounds he stood tall when he would commanded the demons would go into another. Finally, Milton said, "Everybody must leave so the demons won't go into you". Boy! What did he say that for? Folks started running. I saw Carl Barner's five children, all trying to get on his shoulder all at once. It was pandemonium! By this time I am getting in the groove, I have joined Milton in demanding the demons to leave. I saw both sets of those double doors open at the same time with no one there they just swung open and remained for at least fifteen to twenty seconds the demons went out just like that and the girls relaxed proclaiming, thank you Jesus, thank you Jesus but guess what, those demons went next door to the bar and within minutes men came out of the bar fighting in the middle of big Grandriver Street blocking the traffic fighting in the street. One drunk fellow recognized were the demons came from so he was out there in the street hollering don't go to that Church it is full of demons, I am sure he was the devil himself and he know exactly what was happening." These kinds of experiences are sometimes hard to believe, but I have with my own eyes have witnessed these kinds of paranormal spiritual experiences in a black Baptist church. Although these are heard of in many of the spiritual Pentecostal churches, Greater Ebenezer and Pastor Murphy have been placed in the forefront of transitioning many of the Baptist churches to understand the full range of power is available to all churches. God has not only designated power to his body of believers, but he has, we believe given certain assignments to those communities of faith that would surrender their "programs" of orders for services and be open to tap into the shifts he has desired for them. Pastor Murphy moves with the shift:

"O Lord my God, what is happening? O my goodness Lord what are you doing to me? Why is Satan allowed to attack us this way? Believe me I am not sure what the world is happening I didn't know what to do other than pray and that I did; I did not know that God was carrying me to another level of spiritual operation in fact I didn't know anything about what is called another level. I did not know that God had invested in me the kind of power or those spiritual gifts I always thought the ministry was for those saints or church of God in Christ or those sanctified folks, but certainly not for me, the occurrence was so phenomenal that it made me reclaim profession of my conversion salvation anointing and Divine calling. O' Boy I was so glad all of the previous was a miraculous occurrence, I know, I know, I know; and nothing could change me."

"Well Sunday morning the devil would manifest again. One of the choir members during the high of the spiritual worship went under the pews, I was so ashamed I just let her lay there under the pew until I dismissed the service; because I didn't want the members that had not heard about what had happened to know what was going on, so I kept quiet."

"As soon as service ended, I jumped all over Satan with my big shiny cross around my neck and demanding Satan to get going. He left immediately, but O' he would come again the very next Tuesday: we had just finished choir rehearsal when Mrs. Terry called and said, "What in the world have you done to my child Vadie, please come up here and see about her. Mama and I jumped in the car and hurried to their home on Kentucky Street about five blocks behind the Church. When we arrived and went into the house people were standing all around the walls looking at Vadie who was shivering and soaking wet with sweat and half dead. I asked Mrs. Terry to show me to her bedroom and help me carry her there, so we took hold of her, practically dragged her into the bedroom and we put her on the bed. I then asked them to leave, close the door behind them only to leave mama and I. We started reading the scripture. Mama and I started to rebuke Satan speaking with a strong demanding authoritative tone of voice for a while it seemed that Satan wasn't going to flee, but the Holy Spirit reminded me of the cross around my neck. So I raised that cross before her face while holding her hand and arms at the same time making her look at the cross and Satan could not stand the Word mama was reading and me demanding him to leave by the name Jesus Christ of Nazareth his blood. The word was too much for Satan, he had to go; so he left her saying, "Thank-you Jesus, Thank-you Jesus." We then opened the door, and everyone was amazed at the results for there Vadie was standing before them closed in her right mind. Therefore, we Ebenezians kept fasting and praying so Satan stayed away for a while and we moved on in the Holy Spirit, letting God use us to win many souls for Christ, and very soon, the little building was too small. People would come to church and couldn't get in members would stick their envelopes through the door and either go back home or to another Church. The Lord was sending folks from all over the city as a matter of fact, members from other churches would be on their way to their churches and couldn't pass by Greater Ebenezer, and some would just turn into our parking lot. God was adding to the Church daily as he seen fit, as the church grew I kept looking to find a more suitable place to worship even if we had to build. The marathon oil co. gave us the property at Grandriver and Wyoming southeast corner and I acquired an architect designer to build, but the City of Detroit would not let us build because we did not have adequate parking spaces so we had to give the property back. We also purchased property at Meyer's and Grandriver nine lots on the Southwest corner of Meyer's and Grandriver with a nice building on it that we had plains to make a restaurant, the building burned one Saturday so we had to get off of that deal. Mrs. Ford gave us our money back that we had deposited as a down payment so we started looking elsewhere. There was a real estate man, a Rev. Thrasher that called me one Monday morning asking if I would like to see a Church building he had for sale. I quickly said no; I was not interested but he insisted that I see the building he kept explaining the benefits for instance one of the incentives was a daycare of which he suggested would either pay for or at least help pay the note. I finally agreed to see the building, Mrs. Garth, mama and myself went with Dr. Thrasher upon viewing the building I had such admiration and was so elated over the beauty and spaciousness I could see no way we could afford such a mammoth acquisition but mama stood outside of the Pastor's office looking up into the sealing and said honey the Lord just told me this is your Church; I replied you don't say, child we can not afford this place, we were waiting to see the Pastor of the First Church of the Nazarenes who was the sellers I wanted to get permission for our members to see the building and if we could meet that coming Wednesday evening once we were privileged to meet with Pastor Luther he consented, boy, "I was truly inspired, our members would get the opportunity to see the building we met that second Wednesday evening in August 1977. All that met with us was inspired we were also privileged to Congregate in the inner courts of the Sanctuary for meditation and prayers; I shall never forget Rev. Samuel-Turner led the prayer. Dr. Sam Turner prayed until it seemed as is the walls would come tumbling down. In his prayers, he asked God to give us; as he put it this mountain. Pastor Sam Turner prayed, so confidently that when we left all of us felt like that was our building. Saturday evening of the same week, I called a Church meeting to discuss plains and formulate ideas to purchase the building we called for a show of hands of those in favor of moving to that location all present except one was in favor of the move Mother Ruth Andrews and her only reason was she just didn't want to change locations, no harm done of course at this juncture, we were about five hundred members strong or better and did we flex our muscles for that Sunday morning we raised over fifty thousand dollars as honest monies down on the building and we went to work. Mama Murphy, Mrs. Wilma English, Mother Lucile Wilburn, and others started selling chicken and barbeque rib dinners; each and every week putting forth every effort to reach our goal. Mrs. Jacqueline Garth was our secretary at that time, so she and I had the obligation to find the money needed to purchase the building. We went from bank to bank, and how they disappointed Jackie and I we had opened up an account with First independent Bank with the hope that they would help us; the President at the time was a Mr. Washington that guy held us up for four weeks and then called me down there to the bank just to tell me or advise me so he thought that the project was to much for us to handle, he suggested that we should find a smaller building. My my my I refuse to tell you just what I told him, it wasn't good I assure you. Jackie and I then went to National Bank of Detroit. It was at that time the bank manager offered us three hundred seventy five thousand dollars which was not enough to purchase the property. The President of N.B.D. then called First Independent Bank to see if they would loan us the balance. The amount needed was six hundred forty thousand dollars, I knew when the president of N.B.D. called First Independent Mr. Washington would say no, and he did. Jackie and I then went to Manufacture's Bank and filled out an application form there and to no avail, every where went was a dead end, but I continued prayerfully for I was convinced that some way, some how God was going to work it out, all I needed to do was to stay focused and faithful, I was inspired to call the real estate man, the Rev. Thrasher to discuss the situation and he informed me that he could find the money for me for fifty thousand dollars, I thought that was preposterous to give someone fifty thousand dollars but that's what he wanted. Again I went in prayer and the Lord woke me up late one night with a loud voice saying, "I sent Thresher to you in the first place and whatever he say you do it." That was a Saturday night, so I went to the pulpit that Sunday morning and told the Church what the Lord had said other wards the Lord wonted me to give Rev. Thrasher the fifty thousand dollars therefore I had to convince the Church of what the Lord said we must do. The church agreed and we gave Rev Thrasher the fifty thousand dollars and he went to work, in a few days, he called me and gave me the plain First Federal Loans & Savings would let us have four thousand and fifty thousand dollars only we must raise one hundred and ninety thousand dollars. I remember meeting with Pastor Luther and the seller and requesting the brokers fee, which was the monies paid the real estate man present I asked Pastor Luther if I could have that money If I purchased the building and he agreed only I would have to wait until the agents contract expired and that expiration date was July 18, 1977, I waited and Pastor Luther gave me credit for the forty thousand dollars, the asking price for the property was six hundred thousand and forty thousand dollars the bank would only loan us four hundred and fifty thousand dollars, so I went back to Pastor Luther requesting that he loan me a hundred thousand dollars, and he responded to my request in a way that seemed to indicate that I had lost my mind, stating that he could not do that because they needed money from the sale in order to continue their new building which was at a standstill. I then suggested that he give me an affidavit stating that I had a hundred thousand dollars credit with him, have it notarized and the bank would except that affidavit as cash. He then consented to try by meeting with his board of directors for approval and sure enough, it worked, they approved. Now I have one hundred and forty thousand dollars that I need of one hundred and ninety thousand we then set a closing date and all I would need was fifty thousand dollar to close of that amount we scrapped the bottom of the barrel per say trying to raise fifty thousand the balance needed to close, but we could only raise thirty- eight thousand dollars the closing date was upon us and we needed another twelve thousand to reach our goal: my thinking was if we had one more Sunday we could or at least we would have a chance to raise the balance and to do that I would have to post pone the closing date, just so happened that my favorite cousin Louise's husband died and I needed to attend the funeral so mama and I packed up and hit the road: I waited until I was way down in Ohio before calling the sellers to request another closing date on the grounds that I had an emergency so we deferred the closing date another week that would give me another Sunday, and a chance to raise the additional money I needed to close but guess what I could not raise a dime more it seemed no body had any money, so now the closing date is approaching and I am not ready, but God had told me what to do but I was not listening on my way to Memphis the Lord spoke to me and said, "Go to Mr. Hunter, a Detroit business man and ask him to loan you the money." But I didn't pay the voice any attention, I thought it was just something that came into my mind. Mrs. Jacqueline Garth and I went to the close on a Thursday and I wrote the sellers a check for fifty thousand dollars with only thirty eight thousand in the bank on our way down Grandriver I said to Mrs. Garth, "Jackie do you know what I just did?" She said, "Yes you just wrote those people a bad check." We chuckled and went on back to our little church building on Grandriver I went to my office and sat down behind my desk and said with a loud voice, "Lord what am I going to do?" The Lord quickly responded I told you what to do all of a sudden it dawned on me what the Lord had said on my way to Memphis. I then dialed Jackie and asked her to get me Mr. Hunter on the phone she did and I said to him, " Mr. Hunter I need to see you on some business and it's very important", he replied, "I am very busy and I am leaving town in the morning I've got to go to Washington" but "Mr. Hunter I said, I need to see you before you go," he then invited me to come to his office after five o'clock that evening, boy was I relieved. I went by Brother Garth's home and asked him to go with me so he could help me plead our case so he went with me. Finally, when Mr. Hunter could see us, I begin to explain my need by showing the contract transactions etc. My presentation was pretty good for when I finished, Mr. Hunter said, "Well you don't have any collateral," I said, "No sir, everything I have is tied up," he then said, "That's alright, I am going to let you have the money and you have to pay me no interest just pay me back when you get it," the man wrote us a check for twelve thousand dollars no strings attached the Lord made a way and how. Praise God!

We then set the date to move in on the first Sunday, the sixth day of November. We planned a grand occasion, to march from 12000 Grandriver to 18751 Fenkell Ave. The Brown brothers owned a lumber company and there-fore owned a big eighteen wheeler and we built a church choir stand, pulpit area to go on the trailer truck. However that Sunday it rained like never before, so we marched in the rain, everything and everybody got wet, but Oh what a time the man that ordained me for ministry the late Dr. E.L. Slay and the late Coleman A. Young, Mayor of the City of Detroit, cut the ribbon and brought us into the new building. Oh what a time to remember our dedication service was a glorious occasion, we dedicated even the windows, doors, pews, pulpit, choir stand and altar we dedicated everything. My Pastor Dr. Slay was with us the whole week. My, my, how God did add to the church daily. G.E. continued to grow by leaps and bounds and it was necessary, for the bills had to be paid. Would you believe our monthly expense increased by one thousand percent? We really had to make many financial sacrifices to sustain the building, on my first anniversary they raised around twenty six thousand dollars, when I finished paying the bills, I had less than a hundred dollars left and that is the truth the whole truth and that went on for many years when the Church gave me an appreciation, the monies where returned to the church for the furtherance of the ministry of Greater Ebenezer."

This is the unselfish actions on behalf of a shepherd demonstrating his willingness to give of himself until it works out for the glory of God in his life. When Pastor Murphy decided to sacrifice personal gain for the furtherance of Greater Ebenezer Missionary Baptist Church and her ministries, he also calls forth the sacrifices of his family to make as well. His family has also sacrificed many creature comforts and conveniences to help manifest their father's calling upon his life. His family has sacrificed above all the attention and some time they may have desired or needed at times for the sake of the church, namely Greater Ebenezer. All of his children have giving of themselves in so many capacities that there is no place within the foundation and structure of the church that has not been touched by their time, sweat, and tears of joy. His children have been remarkable in their efforts to maintain the Christian integrity it takes to change the "Preacher's kids" modality within the black Baptist church. Teamed with their mother, Momma Murphy, they have risen to many heights of personal achievements and professional prestige, which exemplifies the passion of their former slave grandmother, to make something out of themselves. In my personal encounters and experiences with all of his children, there has not been a moment of conflict or contradiction as to the respect they demanded from others as well as displayed for each other. They too are models of their parents' ambitions to hold family at the highest possible accentuation. Many people have tried to emulate their family structure, however some made it and some did not, but I think after this writing is brought forth, it will empower many to hang tough in difficult times and to be strong in the Lord through it all. The family is still crucial to the survival of the black Baptist church and the community as well. The legacy of the Murphy family will be without a doubt a model of faith for many generations to come, no matter the denominational preference or style of worship, the black Baptist church has been blessed to birth such a family of faith.

Chapter 9.

"Bud" and the Sons of Thunder"

I n the very fiber and fabric of the life of a pastor, there is the often-unique way of speaking into the lives of the people whom you are leading. What matters the most is the words or pet phrases that are used to express potential and possibility that can be seen in their lives. One of the pet phrases that was often used around the Greater Ebenezer was the word "Bud." This was problematic for the author for a number of years and it was taken many times as something negative or disrespectful as well, but while sitting in the classroom of Dr. Pelt's Baptist History class some twenty-five years later, there was a prophetic voice that ranged in the mind and spirit that elevated the true appreciation for the word or name "Bud." Anything that is a bud, has the potential of becoming something; it has possibility and it is full of promise. "Bud" is the embryonic image of the matured intentions of the creature to bloom the fruit he has place within it, the foretaste of the glory that will be revealed, in the days to come. This revelation and illumination struck deep to the core being and it reminds us G.E. "Buds" that we have not yet finished the work for the Lord. Therefore included in this work are the "call to preach" stories and words of wisdom of the sons of Greater Ebenezer and from the loins of William Henry Murphy's ministry.

One the most meaning examples of the transformation that was witnessed at Greater Ebenezer, was that of Elder Darryl Humes. In recollection of my personal witness, Elder Humes was quite the kind of man in his earlier years as a youth deacon and senior deacon, many of us admired. He was always well groomed, highly knowledgeable of the biblical text, and a hard worker. He would at occasion share some intimate moments with me at his parents house that were without reservation a living testimony of his call to the ministry. Many were not surprise when he was called to preach. God had laid a solid foundation in his personhood long before he outwardly expressed his irresistible urge to preach. Elder Humes says this on June 17, 2007

It was the winter of December 25, 1977, that I joined the Greater Ebenezer Missionary Full Gospel Baptist Church. I was nineteen years old, and impressed with the man Preaching, his name was Dr. William H. Murphy, Sr. I know that Dr. Murphy, was the instrument in Gods hand, to bring me to the level of knowledge, and understanding in Christ. Sitting behind his big desk, I would hear some of the most Wisest and inspiring words. He would open the rivers and oceans of proverbs and priceless words.

I can remember him saying, "Son, let's look at the word "TIME". He said there is a time when right is wrong, when done at the wrong Time. I can also remember him saying, "the problem with being both poor and rich". Poor - your outdoors, when you should be Indoors: You're hungry, when you should be full: and you are walking when you should be riding: The problem with being rich Is our misconception of why we are rich? One should be rich for the good of humanity and the relief of the poor. On Saturday's, we would all meet up in our Church Fellowship Hall and listen as

Pastor would talk about God in Christ Incarnation. He said only God could wrap himself up in the **womb of a woman** *for nine month's (asleep) and still rule the world. Finally, as we rode in his car he looks at me and said, "Son" there is a danger in arriving too soon? God knows how much time he will give you to live, so he does not need to get in a hurry To bless you.*

One other such fitting person that falls into this walk of transformation is that of Elder William Reese, Sr.. He has been witnessed by many as one who seeks to follow the Lord's leadings. We were able to slow him down long enough for him to share the following: "*As I look back on time spent as a servant of our Lord with this Man of God, Dr. William H. Murphy, Sr., to state everything that I have learned, the many words of knowledge and understanding of the power and operation of our Trinity God, that would require another separate book. The wisdom and power that God has invested in Dr. Murphy, Sr., can't be explained in mere words. You would have to see it for yourself. In other words, the Holy Ghost would have to reveal it to you, just as he has revealed it to me.*

In 1998, I was serving as a Deacon under Dr. Murphy, Sr.'s leadership. I had been serving in that position since 1983. In 1998, Dr. Murphy, Sr., did not have enough male clergy servants to assist him. One First Sunday Evening, I observed, rather the Holy Ghost showed me how tired Pastor Murphy Sr. was as we were preparing to partake of the of the Lord's Supper. I replied to the Holy Ghost, "I can't go up there to help him. This is as far as I go as a Deacon." Within two-three weeks, the Lord Jesus Christ placed a call on my life to come into the ministry. I accepted God's call. I preached my trial sermon and was later ordained and licensed by Dr. Murphy, Sr."

Today, I serve in ministry full time. I serve as an Assistant to the Pastor. This ministry job entails working 9:00 am-4:00 p.m., Monday-Saturday. Our ministry most times requires that those hours aren't etched in stone. I thank God for the opportunity to serve under Pastor Murphy. Dr. Murphy even now is a hand on Pastor. He visits parishioners in then hospital, performs weddings, and preaches eulogies. This is a rarity for Men of God of his statue in 2007. He is a Man of God driven by divine purpose. Dr. Murphy, Sr. can often be found literally planting flowers and cleaning a toilet. He lives by the creed that, "I'm not going to ask of anyone, what I'm not willing to do myself." Dr. Murphy, Sr. leads by example.

Pastor Kevin Jackson was the very first man to be accepted as a candidate from Pastor Murphy's ministry, for the gospel ministry of preaching. His story in very unique, because it covers a wide range of experience in the trans-formation process. Pastor Kevin Jackson shares his story: *My relationship with Pastor Murphy Sr. is some 30 years plus..., to define it..*

I first encountered Pastor Murphy Sr. in the summer of 1975 at an evening service. It was a sweltering hot late June Sunday evening at the "bank church" on the corner of Grand River and Kentucky in Detroit, the air condi-tioners had not yet been installed. The atmosphere was spiritually charged as there was spiritual determination in every action of the service, the music, the choir, the message, the methods, all possessed a provoking nature; to uplift, to inspire, and to empower. I believe this is one reason that so many preachers and pastors heed our callings at Greater Ebenezer... because Doctor Murphy Sr. creates a spiritual campground for preparation to confront the "wickedness in high places" to be encountered!

My own calling was almost exactly a year later in 1976. Contrary to what I have heard concerning others that have been called under Pastor's "Doc's" ministry, I was not told to "go back!" As I remember, rather his advice to me was to "be very prayerful", advice that has been my standard to this very day!

As I have remarked before, as one of the earliest ministers called from this Greater Ebenezer ministry, I am sure this has caused Pastor to use more high scrutiny in later candidates. More than representing Greater Ebenezer and Pastor Murphy, I believe (I know!), is more concerned with the representation that each minister makes of Christ and "The Church".

Furthermore, Doctor Murphy Sr. is very much the traditional "old school" pastor in this since, upon receiving an offering for his young preachers his advice, as I remember it, was always the same, "Use this offering to buy yourself a good set of commentaries!" Pastor is very much an academic, intellectual preacher. He does not appreciate empty, non-substantive, hollow preaching.

Many church ministries around the community and doubtless the country have benefited from Doctor Murphy's ministry......I am certain that there are those who have passed through G.E. un-introduced and unannounced who were so taken by the presentation of the Holy Spirit in that place that they left and tried to emulate it elsewhere, some successfully, some not! I know for a fact, that some pastors have attempted to emulate aspects of G.E., as well as Doctor Murphy's personality with varying degrees of success and failure....Finally, with all that is known about Doctor Murphy is and will remain an enigma.

Legends are and will be told concerning him. Some will speak of him conversing with and casting out demons. Some will tell of witnessing the lame being restored. Others will tell of great healings and miracles by his Mantle. Some

*will speak of his bold and confident manner. I have been
and still am a witness to all these, as well as many other
aspects of the man and pastor William H. Murphy Sr. some
will believe and some won't. And there is one other thing
that I believe may be well overlooked by many that observe
Doctor Murphy from a pastoral view and that is, with all that
he has and is still in pursuit of accomplishing he possesses
humility not match by many men of this day.*

Pastor Michael Seay is one that exhibits the fine quali-
ties of that of Timothy of the bible. He was a child raised
completely in the ministry of Pastor Murphy. Listen to Pastor
Seay as he shares with us, his story:

*We cannot live for ourselves alone. Our lives are
connected by a thousand invisible threads, and along
these sympathetic fibers, our actins run as causes
and return to us as results.*

—Herman Melville

Dear Pastor Murphy,
*I would like to take this opportunity to say thank you for
being such an integral and inspiring part of my life. Although
it was my mother who planted the seed of God's word and love
inside of my heart, it was you who helped to feed and nurture
that precious gift so that God's purpose for my life would be
revealed. So many times, hi our lives we take for granted the
small things; however, it is those small things that expose our
true compassion and genuine concern for the lives of those that
we meet.*
As a young boy.....; as a young man...As a spiritual leader.
*Respect for you has always been necessary simply because
of your faith in God's word, the consistency of your actions, and
your strong desire to reach and teach all of those who have not
come to know Jesus for themselves. You were never afraid to*

own Jesus before men.....I can still remember when the doors of the church were open and you would ask those in your presence to elevate their right hands if they had 1)Accepted Jesus Christ as their personal savior 2) Been baptized by emersion in water and 3)Attended their church home in the last 90 days. These questions were never to embarrass anyone, but to extend God's love and to offer that precious gift of salvation and eternal life to them.

As Pastor and leader over many, you encouraged the youth to tap into their spiritual gifts and allowed them to express those gifts under the guidance of the Holy Spirit. Your encouragement of spiritual growth of all of the saints undeniably coincides with God's command to go and teach all nations and to teach them to observe all things whatsoever I have commanded you. Your love for God's word was also evident in your own stretching out spiritually and educationally.....in your writing, in your spiritual mission, and in your vision.

Many spiritual relationships were developed in Greater Ebenezer Missionary Baptist church under your spiritual leadership. Wherever members of your flock are teaching, preaching, or serving...the love and sincerity that is generated, is a direct reflection of your anointing, your teaching, and your great leadership.

Pastor Steven Dale King, now pastor of New Canaan Word of God Ministries of College Park, Georgia carries the church planting and mobilization spirit of Pastor Murphy. He has served as pastor in churches in Tennessee and Atlanta, but because of his style of leadership and anointing, God has led him to organize New Canaan Baptist Church and Ministries to re-organize that ministry to shift the focus from the original denominational connection, to a church for the changing of the times. In a telephone interview June 6, 2007 about his call to preach. He was delighted to gives us this up close and personal information: *"I recall on one evening while listening to the trial sermon of a Pastor to be, while sitting in the far back of the sanctuary, Reverend Samuel Berry, Jr., remarked, "King, you will be next." Well it was not long after that when I went into Pastor Murphy's office and shared the burden upon my heart from the Lord. Shortly after that, I preached my trial sermon and diligently worked with and for my pastor. For by trade I am a carpenter and I have always sensed a call to build something with my hands, but God wanted me also to build his people up into the image of his son and our Lord, Jesus Christ from my heart. Therefore, it has been my main objective to take what other people view as just a piece of wood, plank, or a wasted life and in my hands, make it or them into something or someone useful for the glory of the Lord.*

Pastor Alvin M. Ballinger, Sr. pastor of the St. Mark Missionary Baptist Church of Columbus, Ohio, has left his mark on the life of Greater Ebenezer for decades to come. He was the quintessential example of service as a Co-Pastor and employee. He demonstrated the loyalty and confidentiality has not yet been duplicated since. He would serve until late hours of the morning. Often times criticized for being late or tardy, many were unaware of his duties beyond the normal expectations. He exhibited the no quit attitude of his spiritual father, Pastor Murphy. During a long distance phone call on July 26, 2007 at about 11:30am, while traveling through the hill and mountains of Tennessee on I-40 East, I called Pastor Ballinger, and we talked about how much time has passed since we discussed the book project and why I did not have the information we needed from him. He informed me of his work schedule and his redevelopment of the Church's ministry at St. Mark was much like that of the beginning days of G.E. In our conversation, he informed me of this inspiration, that this project could not contain the many wise encounters he shared with our Pastor and that this book would indeed open the door for many others to write their stories. He humbly apologized and made a commitment to support the project further down the line.

Bishop William Henry Murphy, Jr., the only biological son of Pastor Murphy, Sr., is by far the balance of man and spirit, humility and grace, mercy and service, example and execution of leadership, fatherhood, and fathering, visionary and planter, a sower and reaper, and friend and brother. Bishop Murphy, whom I affectionately refer to as my brother and my Bishop, goes from "Billy to Bishop." His transition and transformation is without a doubt, much like that of his father's, yet distinctively different in many aspects. He is given a mindset to tread a course of consecration that would give him his own identity from underneath his father's looming wings. He's Murphy, Jr. and the peer pressure of being a PK was not the life he purposed to emulate. God gave him his own individuality and great respect from his father, that their bond has never loosened its power or grip of respect and honor. It is amazing to witness, for these last twenty-seven, the braiding solidarity of a father and son that is so awe filled that even Bishop allows many of us to call his father "Dad." His security of his relationship with his father is a book all by itself. Bishop Murphy, Jr. gives us this: *"From Billy to Bishop"*

"Growing up in a pastor's family had its good days and its bad days. It was both a negative as well as a positive. Especially when it came to the call that was on my life. One incident that sticks out the most was with a deacon at the First Baptist Church in Millington, Tennessee.

My father had served faithfully there for many years and I remember so well hitting the highway to make the trip with him as he ministered to the saints there. One weekend he decided to go to Michigan to preach and the deacon decided that he was not worthy of the weekly support promised to him. To my amazement, that deacon cursed my mother and put us off the grounds of the church for this. It was at this point in my life that I decided that I would never be a preacher. If this was the way people treated the man of God, then I wanted nothing to do with it. The people could have it and so could God.

For years, my heart remained closed to preaching and being a preacher, but my heart remained open to God. For most of my younger years I could hear and sense that the same thing that was on my father was also on me, but yet because of the earlier experience was not willing to say yes to the Lord's call.

Growing up in the church was even a different experi-ence, which brought to light my closed heart in this area. While singing and directing the choir, many times I would just break out and start preaching. Afterwards, people would make comments declaring "Boy you can preach!" or "Boy, you a preacher!" Of course, I would deny that it was so. There were many times late at night that God would wake me up and I could hear Him saying, "Preach my word." I would either ignore the voice, never really saying no, but in deed, saying "No way." After a while, I began to tune out both the voice of the people and the voice of God.

God has a way of convincing those who are His to do His will. Like Jonah in the belly of the whale for three days, like Paul being knocked from his beast and ultimately changing his name from Saul to Paul, God has His way. His will is done in the earth for those who are truly His.

One day while in revival, I remember it so well, as the great Dr. Oris Mays was preaching; the Lord began again to deal with me. As the apostle John was caught up in the Spirit so was I, and while the preacher was ministering I was unable to move. God had arrested me. While fighting inside with God before the people, I was begging God to let me go and to release me. Nevertheless, he said, "I will not release you until you say yes to my will." God said, "It's my will.", and with tears flowing down my face, I began before all the people to say, "Yes, yes, yes Lord... I'll go; I'll preach your word."

After the calling, the Lord really led me into the ministry of serving. Even though I was leading out in many areas, the ministry was all about flowing in the spirit of servitude. Not that I was trying to serve, but that is the Spirit of Christ that was upon me. It was never about trying to become or trying to obtain, it was always about what God could do through me for the kingdom, so much so, until I was the first janitor of Greater Ebenezer. Even when I left for the pastorate, I was still involved in many of the janitorial aspects of the ministry. It was nothing to be seen mopping floors, cutting grass, fixing faucets, etc. This is who I was. This is what was in me. So consequently, even today as a Bishop, I can still be found many times mopping floors, cutting grass, fixing faucets, etc.

I believe that the man of God released this spirit to me that I was called to serve under. It is said of Elisha that he poured water upon the hands of Elijah. Just like Elisha and Elijah, the same mantle that was upon the man of God was released to the one who served him. It is as if the spirit of William H. Murphy, Sr. rests upon William H. Murphy Jr. just as the spirit of Elijah rested upon Elisha. I believe that holding the office of Bishop has come because of the spirit of a servant that was released into my life at an early age. The scripture declares that he that desires the work of a bishop desire a good work. I was taught to work; not for position, not for fame, and not for fortune, but I was taught to work because this is what Christ did.

The Murphy family is without a doubt a legacy that shares a unique anointing and giftings like none other, however from my personal observation, one of the persons I have been privileged to witness the culmination of the

131

lineage has been in the life of Pastor William H. Murphy, III. His dynamics are without a doubt the polished combination of two sides of grandparents distillation of faith infused into his life. No matter which side of his parents upbringings and surroundings, he has been afforded with both parents and grandparents, living the life of faith and walking with the steady beat of hope that was germinated in the womb of his mother before his debut on planet earth.W3 was called to preach, May of 1991.He preached his trial sermon, July 14, 1991. He was ordained and consecrated as an elder, April 28, 1996 and was installed as Lead Pastor of the dREAM Center Church, April 30, 2006. W3 is an accomplished Psalmist, writer, producer, artist, and an effectual dreamer who believes God for the impossible from man's perspective, but rests in his bosom the possibilities that are giving by Almighty God. Now at the time of this writing, there is not enough room to mention the future of William H. Murphy, IV, for he is at the tender age of twelve years old. He will build from his heritage and continue this walk of faith.

Within the William H. Murphy, Jr.'s family is the outpourings of giftings within his younger children, are the twins of the original "Son of Thunder", namely Devaughn and DeJaughn Murphy. These two gifted men of the Gospel, bring to the Murphy dynasty, a dynamic duo of artistic creativity and diversified musical genius, which will not be duplicated in this lifetime. Now at age twenty-five, they are sought by many venues to share their talents and gifts for the glory of the Lord. They too are actively involved and humbly submissive in service to the Lord at their home church. I have been around these men from the beginning of their lives on this side of glory and I will be looking forward, with tiptoe expectancy what the Lord has in store for this world through them. Their two younger siblings, Brittany and Jasmine are the crowning jewels of grace and elegance.

These two women are from a deep heritage of women, full of the virtues not found in many young women of their times.

Elder Paris Lee Smith, Sr., the author has a wild story of transformation and calling to preach. Many witnesses were they that could see something about this young man. His godmother, the late Marian J. Sanders consistently encouraged his heart about what the Lord had laid upon her heart. She would say that, "God is going to use you to preach to thousands, but not until you go through some tough stuff and not until he gets some mess out of you." This prophecy is yet being fulfilled. Listen to the "Preacha" download this: *"My calling to the gospel ministry was in fact the revelations of God allowing me to preach in my sleep. I went to Pastor Murphy with a concern and burden on my heart. During this time is was terribly upset with the fact that I had lost my love at that time to a lie that was told and the confusion or having no clarity of God calling me to preach. I was in his office having this discussion, when he said, "Son, let's pray and ask God to give you clarity." When we prayed, God illuminated that connection with the power of the Holy Ghost in such a way, we both ran out the office and down the hall shouting and praising God for answering our request. Now there was some anger stirred within me, which developed some disappointment of not being given an opportunity to have a trial sermon. It was in 1983 when we prayed, but I left the faithfulness of the church and hit the streets. I went from am embezzling assistant restaurant manager to modeling men's lingerie, to being a male dancer, to becoming a very depressed, confused young man. It was in early 1986 that God spoke clearly, "Preach my Word or Die!" I shall never forget that dreadful time of my life. I was in the bed with my woman at that time, my oldest daughter's mother, when I began to itch all over my body. We were shacking at her mother's house trying to raise our daughter, when all this was going on. I could not sleep because the itchiness would not stop.*

I got into the shower, changed the linen and then I prayed, after hours of itching to the point of wepts and scars were upon my skin. That night, I heard him completely, "Preach my Word or Die!" I got up and told her what the Lord had said, and left with my stuff. At my first chance, I went directly to Pastor Murphy and told him what the Lord had said to me. He listened, I believe seriously, but he replied, "We'll see Bud." Well in July of that same year, unbeknowingly to me, he and Co-pastors William H. Murphy, J., and Alvin M. Ballinger were already in dialogue about my calling to preach story, when I approached his office door, he invited me in and said, "Bud, you still believe God called you to preach?" I replied with confidence, "Yes I do Sir." Then he said, "Well, good because you are preaching your trial sermon on the last Sunday of August at the evening service. The date was August 31, 1986. The first sermon was from, First Peter, the fifth chapter and the sixth verse which reads, "Humble yourself under the mighty hand of God, that he may exalt you in due time." The title of the homily was, "In Due time." Now this sermon is my life's testimony. Praise God! He is not finish yet.

Elder Alton K. Parks Sr. shares with us this internal burning about the man of God, he writes, *"When I think back to into my ministry under the leadership of Dr. William H. Murphy, Sr. My mine goes back to the tender age of six years old. I remember it was a Sunday morning that I told him that I wanted to help him in the pulpit. He responded by telling me that Dr. Martin Luther King, Jr. was six years old when he preached his first sermon. It was eight years later that I received my calling into the ministry. Pastor Murphy has always made it a point to only bring before the people of God men and women who could help us get to the next place in God.*

We were in a revival and we had Bishop Neil C. Ellis from Nassau, Bahamas. While I was standing in the anointing line, Bishop Ellis and he laid his hands on me and told me I was going to preach the gospel. There was sometime that had passed sine he had spoke those words to me. It was the second Sunday of June 1992 when I received my calling into the ministry. That following Monday I came and told Pastor Murphy what had happened to me that the lord called me to preach. Pastor was sitting in his chair he sat up, leaned back, and said, " Yea, Well what did he say?"

After a few meeting with him trying to put a sermon together he told me he wanted Who, What, When, Where, Why and How. It was the second Sunday in December that I preached my first sermon entitled " Serving God when The Chips are down" and on that night, I received a set of Matthew Henry's. From that, time until now Dr. Murphy has never stopped pouring into me as a son in the ministry. There was a time for about six years he released me to help Pastor Devay Myatt who had no minister's at that time.

Dr. Murphy has taught me how to live and carry myself as a Man of God. He has always told me "Son when you mess up. Tell the people you are sorry and you were wrong, but don't hold your head down come out fighting."

-Elder Alton K. Parks, Sr.-

Chapter 10.

From Faith to Faith

≈≈

The closing remarks of this work are from the well-seasoned experiences of a warrior in the faith. Dr. Murphy opens this dialogue with the signs of the times being before his eyes. With the current events that are daily emerging, life holds for this giant, a keen insight with the mandate still fresh upon his spirit, into the reality of the times. With the daily regimen of pastoral duties, he still keeps a close connection with most parishioners. Pastor Murphy looks deeply within his mind and shares with the world his shift from faith to faith. When faith fully matures, it leaves room for God to reach through the portals of life with reflections poised upon the spirit the recollections of his glorious power active in our lives. Upon the request of the author, he responds with this:

"This present world that we are living in, being terrestrial, temporal, decaying, passing gradually toward weakness, dissolution to become decomposed and corrupting therefore necessitating for undaunted faith for pilgrim travelers. All indications points to the fact of the demise of the world, as we know it. Global warming for instance, is a visible sign of the earth's decay and of course if planet earth is on its death bed as some think, then I am sure that its going to be in for a great repair. The number one reason for saying such, is because the Lord Jesus Christ and the saints are going to live on this planet for one thousands years known as the millennium reign of Christ. I do believe that humanity should strive to be good stewards or good keepers of planet earth in order to preserve its beauty and existence. Otherwise, my thinking is she will be fine being in the hands of God the Creator and Sustainer. The main authority for our observation is the word of God. In the word of God, we have a detailed blueprint for the end time and culmination of this world. Planet earth must suffer preparatory pains leading up to the rapture of the saints. According to 1st Thessalonians 4:16 – 17, therefore the penmanship of St. Luke as is given us St. Luke 17: 22 – 36. The magnitude, of this earth's diversity and perplexity being of such makes it very difficult for one to live here without faith, for one to possess a strong belief in a supreme being could very well mean everything and a religious concept, believing in the Almighty is everything when it comes to real love, peace and happiness. I am truly grateful to my Grandmother for have giving me the God ideology exclusively in that understanding the faith that I needed to make it in life, from faith to faith. I remember when Christ Jesus answered the disciples question concerning forgiveness by telling them that they were to forgive those who trespass against them seven times seven, or as many times as they said I am sorry {the meaning} the disciples were to forgive them; when they heard the response of Jesus they in unison said, "Lord increase our faith." They were readily made to face the challenging reality that it takes. Tough faith for tough times, if one is to live life at its fullest one must do so by faith and knowledge; education is learning how to live life at its best. The more education one acquires and the more faith one possesses, the better one can enjoy life. This I perceived at an early age. I remember so vividly, as if it were yesterday an incident that happened in my life. It was in the heart of winter we had no firewood to burn for heat. So as man of the house at fourteen years of age. I hitched up the wagon with a team of mules and headed for the woods, backed up into a wooded area, where I would most likely find some good firewood. It was afternoon when I started so I didn't have much daylight so I had to hurry. I cut down a tree, which was pretty large; too large for me to lift to the wagon. In order to save time, I tried putting it on the wagon anyway, as I attempted to lift it to the wagon the log wedged my left hand between the wagon bed and the wheel and I could not lift it off with only my right hand. The pain was excruciating to the extent, all I could do was pray and cry, and that I did in a most serious way. I ask the Lord God to give me the strength to lift that log off of my hand, and bless His Holy name, He did, and I was able to lift that three hundred pound log off of my hand praise God! That experience said several things to me, first and foremost it said that I could trust God; secondly, it said that God does answer prayer, and thirdly that God really loves and cares for us. I am sure that was the experience that I needed to go from faith to faith. I would travel highway Interstate 70 – 78 – 55- 40 – 61 – 51, all over the south Tennessee, Mississippi, Arkansas, and Alabama. Wherever duty called, I went. I drove a fifty – five Chevy until the speedometer stopped working at one hundred and eighty – eight thousand miles. Half of the time, I didn't know whether or not I would reach my destination. I could not afford new tires and I had to make out with what I had. I can truly say today we've come this far by faith leaning on the Lord trusting in his Holy Word. He has never failed me yet! Oh, oh, oh can't turn around, we've come this far by faith. Don't be discouraged when trouble gets in your way! He will bare your burdens and heal all misery and strife. I have concluded that every test or trial of faith is designed to increase our faith. Throughout my ministry, I have had to leave or quit my place of employment for the pastoral, and it seemed so foolish at the time to my beloved wife and family who was not aware of what was going on between me and the Almighty God. It was faith-to-faith, statute upon statute, precept upon precept. Faith is one of the heavenly gifts' that's very necessary if one is to please God Hebrews 11:6. Pleasing God by faith in God is the key to everything even the Heart of God, to God's greater riches, prosperity, divine health, divine protection, friends, and love ones, the opening of doors, which no man can close. Pleasing the Almighty God by faith, is a walk on the waters of the Galilean Sea disregarding to the boisterous winds; it is an emphatic, if I may but touch but the hem of His garment, I believe I'll be made whole. It is ten leopard men going to show them-selves to the priest for healing. It is taking up one's bed and walking after being at the pool for thirty – eight years. It is responding to the voice and call of Jesus dead for four days in an unconscious state of existence, from faith to faith. I realize now regardless of how long I have been in the war; and how well I have fought from plantation to the pulpit, and how many battles I have entered and victories I have won, the war still goes on. Even in my old age, the adversary has not ceased to tempt, try, assaults, and abase me. I am fully persuaded that; that which I have committed to Him. He is able to keep it against that day, and even though I am well up in age; nevertheless, my last days shall be my best days and they have yet to come from faith to faith. So I am going to stay in the good fight I am going to finish my course, for there is a crown if righteousness laid up for me, and not for me only but to all them, who love His appearance. Amen." And the beat must go on!

Chapter 11.

And The beat Goes On

And the Beat Goes On...

From my prospective that is, where I stand in Christendom for sixty-nine years. That's how long I've been converted as a Christian or disciple of Christ, and of course called into ministry for fifty-four years, pasturing for fifty-three years, all on a Tuesday. Born on a Tuesday, regenerated on a Tuesday and called to preach the gospel on a Tuesday; Tuesday is my day. Praise God! The beat therefore to me means loving God with all thine heart, soul, and strength. Serving, worshiping, and promoting the advancement of the kingdom of our Lord and Savior Jesus Christ. The beat goes on! And we must work until the day is done, we must work while it is day for night cometh when no man can work. We must always abound in the work of the Lord in as much as we know that our labour is not in vain in the Lord. As servants of the most high God we must cry and cry aloud; sound the trumpet with no uncertain sound. The beat goes on:

On a missionary note:

The harvest is still plenteous and the labours are few. 'Pray ye the Lord of the harvest that he would send more labours into the harvest.' Matt. 9:38. A book I have written by divine inspiration entitled, " Snatching Them Out of the Fire" in which I take much pride because of its title and context St. Luke 14:23. 'And the lord said unto the servant Go out into the highways and hedges, and compel them to come in, that my house may befitted'. The great commission is just as commanding to day as it was over two thousand years ago when Jesus uttered it from Mt. Olive slopes. 'Go ye into all the world teach all nations, teaching them to observe all things whatsoever I have commanded you baptizing them in the name of the Father, and of the Son, and of the Holy Ghost and, lo, I am with you always, even to the end of the world," Matthew28:19-20. The beat goes on. I used Jude 23 as a foundation for my thinking concerning evangelism, which says, "some save with fear others pulling out of the fire hating even the garment spotted by the world." One of the definitions for pulling is to draw toward one, to tug. I truly embrace the eschatological doctrine concerning the end times. One of its most serious discussions is the lineal abode of the righteous and the wicket and the beat goes on.

From an eschatological point of view which is the doctrine of last of final things as death judgment, etc. Emery H. Bancroft D. D. and edited by Ronald B. Mayers, in their book *"Christian Theology"* page 347 and 348,writes about what is called, "The intermediate state of the righteous." The Scriptures teach the existence of both the righteous and the wicked after death and prior to the resurrection. In the intermediate state, the soul is without its permanent body, yet with this state is for the righteous one of conscious joy; for the wicked, one of conscious suffering. That the righteous do not receive their permanent glorified bodies at death is plain from First Thessalonians 4:16,17, and First Corinthians 15:52. Where an interval is intimated between Paul's time and the rising of those who slept. The resurrection is to occur in the future, at the last trumpet: John 5:28-30 - "the hour cometh not "now is". There shall be a resurrection Christ was the first fruit First Cor. 15:20-23).*

The question is than why would an Eternal all wise, infinite God allow or usher in upon those mundane shores a person destined for Hell. Well I do not believe that God is directly responsible my belief is that sin is the cause, especially for the wicked. The Lord Jesus once said of those who betrayed Him, good were it for that man if he had never been born. Mark 14:21, Jesus seem to indicate that He had no control over the life of such an individual, which betrayed Him, So better for him that he had never been born. Where on the other hand the Lord Jesus says of the righteous Rom. 8.-29 for we whom he did foreknew he also did predestinate to be conformed to the image of His Son that he might be the firstborn among many brethren. So then, the foreknowledge of God allows him the opportunity to know the eternal destiny of each and every soul that is ushered in upon these mundane shoes.

Therefore, the beat goes on, of the proclamation mandate of the Gospel of our Lord and Savior Jesus Christ. The beat goes on, woe be unto those who are the called, anointed, chosen, men and women of God if they preach not the gospel The beat goes on as it related to the requirement of steadfastness in the faith and the soberness and vigilant because our adversary the devil is as a roaring Lion, walking about seeking whom he may devour; First Peter 5:8. We must as good soldiers, fight the good fight of faith. There is a Vietnamese proverb that says, "Don't join in a fight if you have no weapons." The more you fight the more you get hurt, he who remains faithful until death shall receive a crown of life that fadeth not away. Rev. 2:10

In summary, I concur with the grand apostle Paul, as He charges his Spiritual son Timothy. First Timothy 1:18-19. This charge I commit unto thee son Timothy, according to the prophecies, which went before on thee, that thou by them mightiest war a good warfare: Holding faith, and a good conscience: which some have put away concerning faith have made shipwreck. Notice Paul "charges" Timothy to follow in his footsteps. The word "commit" usage in banking vocabulary and implies a deposit of something of great value. Timothy was to continue to teach the valuable life-changing truth of the gospel in love while guarding the flock against the teaching of false teachers. Paul had not found such a responsibility to easy. Therefore he reminds Timothy of this fact, encouraging him to "war a good warfare'. Note the two weapons of Timothy's warfare mentioned here. First, faith, which, while not specified certainly implies faith in God and Christ's atoning sacrifice, and faith that this cause is just and right, second, a good conscience, yielding a life and ministry free from both controlling sin and the guilt of that sin. Such a conscience comes from a lifestyle bought into submission to God's word. In fact, this couplet-faith and a good conscience - is said to be "the end of the commandment" First Tim. 1:5, being truly agape love. Note, some had abandoned these vital weapons to their destruction - "shipwreck" of their own faith and the faith of their followers. Nevertheless, such weapons, properly used are "mighty through God to the pulling down of strong holds" II Cor. 10:4.

"The beat goes on", as recorded in John 14-16, many of Christ's last words to his disciples as He was about to leave them regarded abiding, holding on, hanging tough, adapting to the teaching - holding on until death, The word "meno" occurs 18 times in this discourse and is translated not only "abide," but also "remind", "dwell", "continue", and "be present", yet present with them. First, "the Father — dwelleth in me" "I am in the Father, and the Father in me" that is they are one and the same, inseparably abiding together, giving great power to those believing on Him. Furthermore, the spirit of God, the "comforter", will "abide with you forever", even the spirit of truth, whom the world cannot receive - but you know Him; for He dwelleth with you, and shall be in you" I am in my father, and ye in me, and I in you. "Abiding in Him, as we see in this scripture and in verse 7, (as opposed to the tragic end of those who "abide not" Luke 16, brings forth much fruit, and that fruit shall "remain" Lu. 16) There is one requirement - that we keep His commandments (14:23 and 15:10), and if we do so, we will continue" and abide" in His love. These things have I spoken unto you, that my joy might remain in you, and that your joy might befall The beat goes on, not only are we to abide while in this world, but many mansions [same root word meaning abiding place]; I will come again, and receive you unto myself, that where I am, there ye may b also."

I don't know about you brethren but I stand with the great Apostle Paul when I say when my earthly journey here is ended, when my mission work is done my calling to fulfill, III bid fare-well to every fear and wipe my weeping eyes. I have fought a good fight I have kept the faith and there is a crown laid up for me of righteousness which the righteous judge shall give me at that day and not to me only but to all those who love his appearing. Amen.

Pastor Murphy's Critiques

In the Intro instead of using hypothetical put in Visionary *(A visionary view of the possibilities...)*

What is the Vision for Ministry?
It is the salvation of lost souls to become citizens of heaven through intercessory, sacrificial and meditorial office of the Son of God, Jesus Christ our Savior.

What is the Vision for the Church?
It is to become a church without spot or wrinkle, the church that has been transformed by the anointing of the Holy Spirit. Adherence to the word of God to be conformed to the image of Christ Jesus.

What vision are we following?
We are following the vision of God for the perfecting of the saints, for the work of the ministry, for the edifying of the body of Christ to bring us all to the unity of the faith, and of the knowledge of the Son of God, unto a perfect man, unto the measure of the statues of the fullness of Christ.

Appendix

"An Uncompromising Research Paper of Black Baptist History: "A Rich Heritage and Worship Experience through the Eyes of a Baptist"

(Submitted to Professor Dr. J. Sherman Pelt By Paris Lee Smith, Sr., for Denominational History: Baptist 30203 ITEH 658 –B Interdenominational Theological Center Atlanta, Georgia December 6, 2005)

Introduction

B aptist Church history is a rich and deeply immense history that is always in need of expression and explanation. One aspect of the Baptist church history is the unique history of black Baptist. The black Baptist church has survived many trials and tribulations from its birth until this present day. The black church is without a doubt, still vibrant in the context of our community. It is through the lenses of this student of Baptist history and the black Baptist church that fortifies this effort to share a not so popular encounter with a world that may never know of this rich history of its transforming message. The debt that is owed to the history of the black Baptist church is being shared with a new generation of black Baptist as they continue to pave the way for others to embrace the richness of their religious experience. This black Baptist history is very mindful of its beginnings that were handed down from the slavery era, yet it has transformed the impossibilities of that era into a rich heritage and history. An era that was laced with torment, terror, and treacherous treatment of black people that the collective religious worship experiences molded by these times shed light on the black Baptist church. Even in the spirituals that they sang, there was a sense of a panacea thematic flow from their souls. Mitchell says, "They foresaw the day when the preachers would fold their Bibles because the last soul would be converted. This Lord they loved so much was coming back, to wake the nations underground. Obviously this was a new theological concept for Africans, but once they found it in Christian teachings, they radically adapted to themselves."[1] James Cone, one of the fathers of Black Theology says that the Spirituals must no longer be look at as some opiate to soothe the pains of the realities endured by the slaves, but must be examined in the light of really meeting the needs of the people who express their soul's cry unto God. Cone says Black slaves were condemned to live in a society where not only the government but "God" condoned slavery. The spirituals were created out of that environment. If black history were no more than the story of what whites did to blacks, there would be no spirituals. Black history is also the record of black people's resistance, an account of their perceptions of their existence in an oppressive society. What whites did to blacks was secondary. The primary reality is what blacks did to whites in order to delimit the white assault on their humanity.[2]

[1] Henry Mitchell, *Black Church Beginnings*: "The Long Hidden Realities of the First Years" (Wm. B. Eerdmans Publishing Co.: Grand Rapids, MI / Cambridge, UK 2004) pg.44

[2] James Cone, The Spirituals and the Blues (Orbis Books: Maryknoll, NY 10545, 1972, reprinted 1991) pg. 23

We are fortunate as a people of color to have a jewel in our community that fills the void that is so needed to be filled and that still shines as a beacon of light and hope to all. This one such jewel of the black community, the black Baptist church, has been afforded to this context the birthing of beginning in the experience of the writer whose own experience is richly rooted in the black Baptist church, unknowingly connected to the ministry of the late Rev. C.L. Franklin. Through the information given to the writer from his mother and uncle, his family was deeply connected to the fiery preacher and his grandmother served as an usher in the New Bethel Baptist Church at its' Hastings' Street location. In the forefront, there is a bias toward the black Baptist, whereas the experiences of the black Baptist church is embedded in the spirit of the writer with great respect to other black experiences in their church context, yet we can truly speak from real experience, with the emotion that will give this project it's magnitude.

The history of a great black Baptist church lies in the bosom of a sharecropper's grandson in the foothills of the Tennessee valley. Such is the person of William Henry Murphy, Sr. His formal education was cultivated in the home of his paternal grandmother whose desire for her grandson, was to make something significant out of his life. At the tender age of seven years old, he became the head of the house, sort of speaking. He was infused with the principles of God concerning integrity, excellence, and reverence. He was raised in the fiery experience of the black Baptist church. His incubated experience cultivated in the south regions of the countryside fields in the valley of Tennessee, he shares his story. It is this Black Baptist history and heritage that meets destiny within the transformation and the thorough under-standing of the black Baptist church history that motivated and inspired this man to lead a life that reaches until this very day. In his experience and context, he has internalized the trials and triumphs with the black Baptist church. His pain and praise lies within the turbulence and tribulations as he lifted and raised the blood stained banner of hope and justice in the midst of the church life. From his humble and fiery exposure of being a field hand on the sharecropper's plantation, not so shortly on this side of slavery, picking cotton and vegetables, and hearing the spiritual hymns of his grandmother singing; working from sun up to sun down, he lives now in the golden years of his life, actively with the work ethic embedded in his bosom from birth he leads a great Black Baptist church in the city of Detroit, Michigan, named Greater Ebenezer Missionary Baptist Church at the age of seventy-nine.

From childhood, he saw the black Baptist church survive many ups and downs, as well as the praise and pitfalls of his own context. He shares this rich history with a son, whose own Baptist upbringings are from the bosom of this black Baptist preacher, wisdom teacher, writer, prophet, historian, and inventor. Countless events and golden nuggets of experience over twenty-five years of being a black Baptist son and preacher, the author shares his view of this black Baptist experience in the reality of the power of the transforming message of the black Baptist church. It is this power of the black Baptist church that the world itself has seen as a model of faith and fortitude that it can and will survive until the day of the Lord's returning. Dr.William Henry Murphy, Sr., inspiring preaching and teaching has lead thousands upon thousands to hear the gospel of transformation, reconciliation, and kingdom living in the set atmosphere of his home church, Ebenezer Baptist Church in Memphis, Tenn., his pastorates of the First Baptist Church of Millington, Tennessee, Brown's Creek Baptist Church of Brownsville, Tennessee, Prince of Peace Baptist Church of Detroit, and now the Greater Ebenezer Missionary Baptist Church of Detroit. Although many times misunderstood by those closes to him, Dr. Murphy's undaunted faith and perseverance and tenacity to keep marching on is heard in a sermon he shared with the historical Council of Baptist Pastors of Detroit and Vicinity at their weekly session at the preaching hour "To Late to Quit."[3] He shares with the seasoned veteran Pastors in preaching that "God has not shut out the lights of hope, although aging and still on the battlefield for the Lord, God still gives marching orders to still fight on. Retirement is not an option. What does a preacher retire from serving the Lord Jesus? Where can he go from God to relax when the fire is still shut up in his bones? How can he tell God that enough is enough? If God is still waking us up every morning, then he has given us another chance to share the gospel story of good news, 'because it's too late to quit."[4] This slogan, "it's too late to quit" is what can be conceived as to what could have been burning in the bosom of the slaves, as they were challenged with the survival of their religious experience and expression. He has taught Mid-week bible studies, new members' membership classes, Baptist Training Union, baptized thousands and has shared Holy Communion with as many, in his unique style, he manages to still give time to all in their need. He provided the sacredness of the black Baptist church in such a way that as a young man the author was privileged to work and learn in the black Baptist church the importance to stand in the church with a sense of holy discontent and reverence that this is the place of the most High God. The black Baptist church is not by some accident, it is divinely appointed by the God of all creation and with a unique style of proclamation, and it has a voice like none other. Its voice is distinguishably different from others in that it resounds with the thunder of heaven and majestic voice of the heavenly host. The black Baptist church is still used as a vehicle of God's voice to the world. This is true

[3] Morning conversation in the office prior to leaving G.E. July 3, 2005.

[4] Sermon preached at the Council of Baptist Pastor of Detroit and Vicinity, July 3, 2005.

and authentic Baptist history, because most Black Baptist history is embedded in the gift that God has given to it from the perspective of the power of the pulpit. Most of the real true history has not been given the adequate space that it is due in the history of the black church in these United States of America. The black Baptist church has had a great impact upon the spiritual and social context of the black church. It is from the pulpit and the pew that the black Baptist church has transformed and transcended the obstacles and opposition to its existence into a ray of hope.

James Melvin Washington writes that from the existence that there was the need for separate congregations from those of the slave owners, the black congregants sensed a deep need to form their own place of worship and religious expression which still embraced their heritage and cultural background that black Baptist churches began to develop all around the areas of Virginia, The Carolinas, Georgia, Florida, Alabama and other regions.[5] Mechal Sobel writes, "That the founders of the black church movement were strong believers in religious freedom. They led black folk in affirming what they believed to be the natural, God-given right to be free. But this was not a notion of freedom without responsibility. Souls had to be saved, brothers and sisters in bondage had to be liberated, and churches had to be organized and built."[6] It is this freedom that Dr. Murphy was thrown out of the Prince of Peace Baptist Church of Detroit, Michigan in 1971. According to Carolyn Johnson a former member of the church, "Pastor Murphy stood up against those deacons who wanted to control everything and every-

---

[5] James Melvin Washington, *"Frustrated Fellowship: The Black Baptist Quest for Social Power"*, (Mercer University Press, Macon, Georgia 31207; originally printed 1986: reprinted 2004) pgs. 11-23

[6] Mechal Sobel, *Trabelin' On: The Slave journey To An Afro-Baptist Faith* (Westport, CT: Greenwood, 1979)

body. They did not like the fact that Pastor Murphy's' style of Pasturing was led by the non- traditional way of their thinking. He insisted that they had an obligation to provide for the pastor and his family and they should be held accountable for their actions to the pastor or the under shepherd of the church." Dr. Murphy has an unbelievable desire for souls to be saved in that its like a fix for a junky hooked on substances, he gets a certain heavenly high when someone confesses the Lord Jesus Christ as Savior in the openness of witnesses at G.E. and other places he is unctioned to share the gospel story.

Everett C. Goodwin in his comments of introduction states, "The Baptist spirit of independence encourages Baptist people to think and act both theologically and personally. So long as the Baptist spirit is alive, those who in some way define themselves within its ranks will wrestle with the personal and public issues of life as if they matter to their faith experience because they are convinced they do."[7] It is this Baptist spirit that will bring forth some unpleasant temporary events, which will provide room for new beginnings to spring forth. One very unique distinctive about Dr. Murphy and G.E. is the Baptist spirit of freedom and the notion that God has not called us to bondage but to liberation and reconciliation.

The spirit of the black Baptist church lives in the fabric of G.E. in that there have always been other winds of tradition and contemporary trends that have beckon the bosom of this great church. Such weathering of the storms of life, G.E. has been a place of reconciliation, which is practiced by Dr. Murphy in all areas of the ministries of the church. The Dr.

---

[7] Everett C. Goodwin, *Baptists in the Balances: The Tension between Freedom and Responsibility*, Introduction to Part V (Judson Press: Valley Forge, PA 19482, 1997) pg. 311

C. Eric Lincoln captures this spirit in his work, "This Road Since Freedom", in the poem entitled, "Reconciliation":[8]

Walk in the light at last

Give me your hand, my brother
Give me your hand
Divided we fall, my brother
Together we stand.
Come, let the night be past
Now is the time to cast
Our lot as one

The quest for freedom will bring forth the necessity to speak out against oppression of any sort. Sometimes when a black person in general speaks up and out it is not always out of arrogance or conceit, but it is from the context to which they have been cultivated and the painful experiences of the past. Racism has been one of the silencers of the black church and when a man whose cultural upbringing was just shy of slavery as lawful, then it is understood and clearly seen as to why Dr. Murphy had to speak up and out about how things at Prince of Peace Baptist Church were reflections of sharecropper field hands mentality. When he spoke up and voiced his God inspired vision for the church this caused a great division in the church and with fifty-four members, including his family, broken and emotionally bruised, spiritually devastated and with the promise of God, the birthing of Greater Ebenezer Missionary Baptist Church.[9] This frustration in the fellowship can become the common denominator to the many births of churches. Pregnant with the promises of God and the obligation to lead

[8] C. Eric Lincoln, *This Road Since Freedom* (Carolina Wren Press: Durham, North Carolina 1990) pg. 10

[9] Conversation at lunch with Dr. Murphy in 1990.

people to a deeper understanding of God's love and concern for his children, Dr. Murphy gathers with those fifty- four souls in prayer and supplication unto the Lord and out of his spiritual loins, a baby is born. A baby whose tender upbringings are unique and essential to its survival, that from the very milk of the Gospel, it is nurtured in the whirlwind of religious uncertainty, it grows as a root in dry places. A root, that grows deep into the history of the black Baptist church. Although not always connected to other churches, Greater Ebenezer Missionary Baptist Church stands alone at times for the uncommon virtues, which started the quest for social freedom and identity. This child of God, Greater Ebenezer takes on the world in so many ways that even until this day its magnitude of impact on the kingdom will not be realized until she gets to glory. Why speak of a church as a child growing up? It is in this perspective that we must look at the church because as Dr. Murphy would inform the writer while cleaning up the bathrooms of the church as a janitor, "Bud, remember you are working for the Lord and God is looking for excellence in all we do in his name and at his church."[10] He believes that the church is still maturing and those who were a part of her rich history and heritage must work in the church for her future end, to be presented as a bride without spot, wrinkle, or blemish. He wanted all to perceive that if the Lord descended from heaven right as he was speaking he wanted the approval of God that the house of worship was clean for his Holy presence to dwell therein. The name "Bud", was offensive to the writer because for many days, he felt a bit of lost identity with the D.O.C. and because of the reverence he had for this man of God, the writer never questioned the pastor on this issue. But as we reflect upon the "Bud" issue, it was in the beginning of this work about black Baptist history, which the writer understood that he was not yet at full bloom, to be identified with where the

[10] Conversation with Dr. Murphy in 1981.

Lord was taking him to according to the eternal destiny. So he is a bud. Bud means alive and promising, full of possibilities. The theology of bud is where the black Baptist church is the fruit of the roots that spring up from dry ground. Dr. Murphy is one of those roots and the writer is as well, but one root nurtures another. The stronger helps the weaker and the wiser helps the foolish. Sometimes there is the need for pruning, so that the root can bare more fruit. Pruning can be painful and productive. Pruning can be lonely and lamenting upon the bosom of the root because the manifestation of the gardener is not always seen immediately. The problem with understanding the pruning procedure, is that the roots has no control over the process to which God has designed for the root to bare more fruit, and in the weakness of the flesh, God perfects the roots to bare more fruit. This pruning for Dr. Murphy has been and continues to be the child he birthed from his spiritual loins, Greater Ebenezer. She helps him to see that growing up in the Lord is not always pleasant and peaceful, but it is rewarding. From leaky roofs to hard -headed members, God prunes Dr. Murphy. From unfaithful ministers to power hungry leaders, God still prunes Dr. Murphy. From jealous preachers to wicked witnesses, God still prunes Dr. Murphy.

In the heart of this Pastor, there is the pains of a Pastor and the burdens of a Bishop, he has endured as a man of God and yet a man of flesh and bones. He has had to be forced to deal with the misunderstandings of family, friends, followers, fellowships, and foes. He shares his black Baptist history in the context of being judged by those he loves the most and he is often times measured by the rise and fall of attendance on Sunday morning. Because he is a lover of God's people, he himself has been subjected toward temptations that have caused him more pain that can be imagined. Being doubted of the promises of God, he has carried the load with God, a black Baptist church through the storms of life amidst being ridiculed concerning his activities with those he has tried to help. Doubted by those of his household and colleagues at times in general, he has stood alone with the promise of God radiating in his bosom. He has kept his promise to God to be faithful to his family but understanding that he could not be flawless at all times. Faithful means that we get back up after we fall down, no matter how many times we fall. Yet he has failed many times with family, friends and the fellowship, he still rises. He heard the Lord tell him to get back up in Tennessee, get up at the Peabody Hotel as a busboy during a crucial racial time in his life, he heard get up during the time Prince of Peace put him out with a wife and six children, and he has heard the words get up all of these years as Pastor of Greater Ebenezer. He hears in the ear of his heart, "Lo I am with you always, even until the end of the world," which has helped him to understand, now well seasoned in years with the Lord and life that grace has kept the steady beat of his soul to keep going in spite of what others feel or can say. He sees mercy as what God has used to help him hold on to the promises he gave him back in the hot fields of Tennessee.

Although out of his spiritual loins there are to this day eight churches, Greater Ebenezer is still mother to them all, but primer to the Pastor. God is still working in the life of this Pastor and in the preparation of this daughter, Greater Ebenezer. This child of God is being matured to stand tall for God long after Pastor Murphy is received in the heavenly places. Therefore the ministry of Pastor Murphy, Sr., will outlive him in days, but also will continue to produce more fruit because of this promise, "Upon this rock I build Greater Ebenezer, and the gates of hell shall not prevail." Come what may, the history of the black Baptist church will be continued until the coming of the Lord Jesus!

"A Casual Essay of Dr. Henry H. Mitchell's "Black Church Beginnings: Seeking a Thorough Perspective for Reflective Engagement"

(Submitted to Professor Dr. J. Sherman Pelt by Paris Lee Smith, Sr. for Denominational History: Baptist 30203 ITEH 658 –B Interdenominational Theological Center Atlanta, Georgia October 31, 2005)

The black Christian church has many debts it owes to the work of the preacher/ teacher and scholar. The black church with its unique dynamic and fortitude is set as a legacy for the African- American race and cultural being. The black church still holds its magnetic force and its shining emblem of God's grace. The black church, the jewel of the black community still manages to stand tall amidst the wind-storms and whirl winds that this society plunges its way. The black church the anchor to the black community seems to have lost its significance with the upwardly mobile blacks who find it convenient to side track the very institution of the black community that fueled and financed their educa-tional pursuits and academic achievements, as well as their economical status.

The black church has an essential rich history that is a part of the African-American history motif that must be given the respectful place in the study of history, especially church history. After reading the classic work of the late Dr. C. Eric Lincoln's, "The Black Church since Frazier," there etched in the heart of my spirit the need to look for the resources as to the why was I placed in the context of the black church, particularly the black Baptist church. In the preface of Dr. Lincoln's collaborative work, "The Black Church in the African American Experience," he says "the burden of the conventional views regarding the Black Church and black religion has to do with the uncritical assumption that the black experience in religion is but the replication of the white experience, shadowed by an African patina predisposing it to an inordinate exoticism and emotionalism which distorts to a significant degree the proper expression of the faith."[11] Dr. Henry H. Mitchell tackles in my opinion this element of exoticism and emotionalism with a vivid discourse of history that puts more substance in the why of the black church and its enormously rich and penetrating heritage. Its penetration is so deep in that as we search for meaning and dialogue, there is the noticeably, overlooked or the untapped reality that the black church is still full of the African traditional religious experience.

Dr. Mitchell, with the help of researchers and scholars in there in own right, offer to us the challenge of upholding this rich history with some integrity and with some sense of direction for our aiding the rest of the black church to not become so sedated with the interpretation of our experience through the lens of other cultural eyes with their optic nerve only sensitive to their own understandings and their retina focused upon what they choose to offer the world for the black church. We are more than a mimic religious experience; we are more than emotionalism displayed on the stage of Sunday mornings, we are a people with a unique in tuned touch with the Almighty creator and God of this age and ages to come. We are the people whose God encounter is clear and vivid, in that no matter what time span or systematic denial of who we are cannot be totally diminished by those who are intimidated by our creative expression of worship or our forcefully excited way of showing our appreciation for the God who has held our hands and hearts down through the years. The black church has evolved into a recognizable viable institution of the black religious life with its innate

---

[11] C. Eric Lincoln and Lawrence H. Mamiya, "The Black Church in the African American Experience" (Duke University Press, Durham and London 1990) pg. xi.

ability to survive the criticisms of the world. The church has endured many popular and unpopular trends as it has grown and matured in it's seeking to be established and recognized as a meaningful experience. The debt that is owed to the many women whom preached and carried many meetings to the saving of souls in the rural areas of these founding historical denominations is phenomenal, if not amazing. The contributions of women are still felt and are still very effective today in the context of church in general. The role of women in mainline black churches is not to be side swiped by traditions that are not founded upon the accurate data. Women are the brace and sometimes the backbone to most denominations.

The black church is still nurtured by the breast of the black women that make the church vital to the social context to which she is called to address and administer to. The survival of the black church is still based upon it knowing its rich history without the distortions that the male dominated perspective has infused into its mind to only believe that a man is the best-qualified individual to lead the black church. Can we rightfully deny the enormous contributions of the black woman to the black church? Can we continue to survive as a black church without thoroughly knowing our history and our focus for the future? Does gender muscle has to be flexed, in order to be a church or can we allow our best and brightest to launch us to the next level regardless of their gender? These are the questions that are affecting the black church. While we are wrestling with the gender of the leadership of the black church today, the black community is being lost to the pantheism and nartistic disease that is causing the community to divide and become conquered by others whose self-interest is how large a bank account they have and property they can secure for their self-aggrandizement. Many have invaded the black community with the disguise of wanting to give to the black community yet

with the backdrop of employment and economic empowerment, they have yet to transform the community. The black
church must return to the black community with a sense of
urgency and sense of sincerity towards the holistic view of
a balanced community within the beloved community in the
book, "Search For The Beloved Community: The Thinking
of Martin Luther King, Jr.", written by authors Kenneth L.
Smith and Ira G. Zepp, Jr., share the thinking and thought
pattern of one the greatest leaders to and from the black
church and black community. In their observations, they
walk through the mind and concepts of King to offer to us
the shaping elements to his vision of a beloved community.
King's conception of the "Beloved Community" is best
described as a transformed and regenerated human society.
King conceived the "Beloved Community" in terms of an
integrated society wherein unity would be an actuality in
every aspect of social life.[12] This is the mindset that launch
forth the whole backbone of the civil rights movement
through the black church and the black community. Yet it
was the balance of man and woman, the black man the black
woman, not exclusively, but inclusively the men kept the
cadence but the women kept the rhythm alive. Movement
for the transformation of the black community, will be the
evidence of concerted efforts that must call forth the black
church to reposition herself at the forefront of the transformation by a prophetically call for a radical, bold, courageous,
and cutting edge mindset to do all that can be done for all of
the community.

---

[12] Kenneth L. Smith and Ira G. Zepp, Jr., Search for the Beloved
Community: The Thinking of Martin Luther King, Jr., (3rd edition,
Judson Press, Valley Forge, PA 19482-08510 pg.130.

Notes

Gerald Lamont Thomas, *"African American Preaching: The Contribution of Dr. Gardner C. Taylor,"pg.7*

Eric Lincoln relates in his book entitled *"Coming through the Fire"* Pgs. 22 –25

Poem written by the late William Herbert Brewster, "I'm Determined To be Somebody, Someday" (The Resolution of the Negro Youth)

Paul Tillich, *"The Courage To Be,"* The Ontology of Anxiety, *pg. 32*

Ibid. pg. 78

The Bible, King James Version, *The Thompson Chain Reference Bible*, Fifth Improved Edition, pg.1265

Dubois' Writings *"The Soul of Black Folks," pgs.398-399*

Cleophus J. LaRue, *"The Heart Of Black Preaching"*, Introduction

Henry H. Mitchell, *"Black preaching: The Recovery of a Powerful Art"*, pg.34

William H. Myers. *"The Irresistible Urge To Preach"*: *A Collection of African American "Call" Stories*. Pg. xxii in preface.

Ibid, pg. xxiv of preface

Gerald Lamont Thomas, *"African American Preaching: The Contribution of Dr. Gardner C. Taylor,"pg.7*

C. Eric Lincoln, *"Coming Through The Fire",pgs. 21-25*

Na'im Akbar, *"Breaking the Chains of Psychological Slavery,"* pg. 31

Dr. Cornel West, in his book, *"Prophesy Deliverance: An Afro-American Revolutionary Christianity pg. 35*

Dr. Cornel West in his phenomenal book, *"Race Matters"* says this as it pertains to leadership, *"Quality leadership is neither the product of one great individual nor the result of odd historical accident. Rather, it comes from deeply bred traditions and communities that shape and mold talented gifted persons."pg56*

Warren H. Stewart shares this with us from his book, *"Interpreting God's Word in Black Preaching"* "The Word can only be identified with and experienced when it be understood... preaching, then, must communicate the Word in the common tongue of those to whom the message is directed.....he or she who is involved in effective and accurate hermeneutics in preaching must not confuse his or her primary assignment with that of the theologians and biblical scholars...the preacher must be an effective translator of the Word of God or else his or her mission will be defeated immediately after the text is read." pg 53.

Emery H. Bancroft D. D. and edited by Ronald B. Mayers, in their book Christian Theology page 347 and 348

The Intermediate State of the Righteous

1. The soul of the believer, at its separation from the body, enters the presence of Christ. (2 Cor. 15:1-8; Luke 23:43)
2. The Spirits of departed believers are with Christ. (Hebrews 12:23; Eccl. 12:7)
3. The state of the believer immediately after death is greatly to be preferred to life in the body upon the earth. (Philippians 1:23)
4. The departed Saints are truly alive and conscious. (Matt. 23:32; Luke 16:22,23:43 ["with me" = in the same state]; Thessalonians 5:10
5. Departed believers are in a state of rest and blessedness. (Rev. 6:9-11,14:13)

The Intermediate State of the Wicked

1. They are in prison, that is, are under constraint, and guard First Peter 3:19. There is no need of putting unconscious spirits under guard, restraint implies the power of action.
2. They are in torment, or conscious suffering. (Lu. 16:23)
3. They are under punishment. (Heb. 9:27)

Bibliography

Na'im Akbar, Ph.D., "Breaking the Chains of Psychological Slavery" (Mind Productions and Associates, Inc. Tallahassee, Florida 32304 1996)

Emery H. Bancroft, "Christian Theology, Systematic and Biblical" 2nd edition (Zondervan Publishing House, Grand Rapids, MI 1976) pgs. 47-348

George Barna and Harry R. Jackson, Jr. "High Impact African-American Churches" (Regal Books, Ventura, California 2004)

James Cone, The Spirituals and the Blues (Orbis Books: Maryknoll, NY 10545, 1972, reprinted 1991) pg. 23

E. Franklin Frazier, "The Negro Church in America"; C. Eric Lincoln, "The Black Church Since Frazier" (Schocken Books Inc., New York 1974)

Everett C. Goodwin, *Baptists in the Balances: The Tension between Freedom and Responsibility*, Introduction to Part V (Judson Press: Valley Forge, PA 19482, 1997) pg. 311

Cleophus J. Larue, "The Heart of Black Preaching" (Westminster John Knox Press, Louisville, Kentucky 40202-1396 2000) pg.34

C. Eric Lincoln, *This Road Since Freedom* (Carolina Wren Press: Durham, North Carolina 1990) pg. 10

C. Eric Lincoln, *"Coming Through The Fire"*(Duke University Press, Durham, North Carolina,1990),pgs. 21-25

C. Eric Lincoln and Lawrence H. Mamiya, "The Black Church in the African American Experience" (Duke University Press, Durham and London 1990)

Henry Mitchell, *Black Church Beginnings*: "The Long Hidden Realities of the First Years" (Wm. B. Eerdmans Publishing Co.: Grand Rapids, MI / Cambridge, UK 2004) pg.44

Henry H. Mitchell, "Black Church Beginnings: The Long-Hidden Realities of the First Years" (William B. Eerdmans Publishing Company, Grand Rapids, Michigan/Cambridge, U.K. 2004)

Henry H. Mitchell, "Black Preaching: The Recovery of a Powerful Art" (Abingdon Press, Nashville, TN 37203 1990)

Marvin A. McMickle, "Preaching to the Black Middle Class: Words of Challenge, Words of Hope" (Judson Press, Valley Forge, PA 19482-0851 2000)

William Henry Murphy, Sr., (pastor of the Greater Ebenezer Missionary Baptist Church, Detroit, Mi) Collective conver-

sations from 1981- until present. Sermon preached at the
Council of Baptist Pastors of Detroit and Vicinity, July 5,
2005, Dr. Bullock is President.

William H. Myers, "The Irresistible Urge to Preach: A
Collection of African American "Call" Stories" (Aaron
Press, Publishers, Atlanta, Georgia 30309 1992)

J. Deotis Roberts, "Africentric Christianity: A Theological
Appraisal for Ministry" (Judson Press, Valley Forge, PA
19482-0851 2000)

Mechal Sobel, *Trabelin' On: The Slave journey To An Afro-
Baptist Faith (*Westport, CT: Greenwood, 1979)

Kenneth L. Smith and Ira G. Zepp, Jr., Search for the Beloved
Community: The Thinking of Martin Luther King, Jr.,
(3rd edition, Judson Press, Valley Forge, PA 19482-0851)
pg.130.

Warren H. Stewart, Sr., "Interpreting God's Word in Black
Preaching" (Judson Press, Valley Forge, PA 19482-0851;
Second Printing 1988

Paul Tillich, "The Courage to Be" (New Haven and London
Yale University Press1980)

Gerald Lamont Thomas, "African American Preaching"
The Contribution of Dr. Gardner C. Taylor, (Peter Lang
Publishing, Inc., New York, New York 2004)

James Melvin Washington, *"Frustrated Fellowship: The
Black Baptist Quest for Social Power"*, (Mercer University
Press, Macon, Georgia 31207; originally printed 1986:
reprinted 2004) pgs. 11-23

Cornel West, "Prophesy Deliverance: An Afro-American Revolutionary Christianity" (The Westminster Press, Philadelphia, Pennsylvania 1982) pg. 35

Cornel West, "Race Matters" (Vintage Books, New York 1994) pg.56

William H. Willimon and Richard Lischer, "Concise Encyclopedia of Preaching" (Westminster John Knox Press, Louisville, Kentucky 40202-1396 1995)

The Bible, King James Version, *The Thompson Chain Reference Bible*, Fifth Improved Edition, pg.1265

Printed in the United States
90100LV00002B/19-168/A

9 781604 771060